D0416985

MOUNT LONDON

Edited by Tom Chivers & Martin Kratz

TOM CHIVERS was born in Herne Hill, south London in 1983. His publications include *How to Build a City* (Salt, 2009), *The Terrors* (Nine Arches, 2009), *Flood Drain* (Annexe, 2014) and, as editor, the anthologies *City State: New London Poetry* and *Adventures in Form* (Penned in the Margins, 2009 & 2012). He has made site-specific, perambulatory and audio work for Southbank Centre, Bishopsgate Institute, the Eden Project and LIFT. An award-winning independent arts producer, he is former co-Director of London Word Festival and currently runs Penned in the Margins from a small office in Aldgate. He lives in Rotherhithe.

MARTIN KRATZ is an associate lecturer in English at Manchester Metropolitan University. His poetry has been widely published in magazines including *The Rialto, Magma, The Interpreter's House* and *The Moth*. As a librettist, he collaborates regularly with the composer Leo Geyer, and their projects include the prizewinning song cycle *Sideshows*. Their chamber opera *The Mermaid of Zennor* was described by *The Times* as 'imaginative and beautifully shaped.'

MOUNT LONDON

Ascents in the Vertical City

To Nick,

REACH FOR THE TOP
OF THAT MOUNTAIN!

Amber xx

Penned in the Margins

LONDON

PUBLISHED BY PENNED IN THE MARGINS
22 Toynbee Studios, 28 Commercial Street, London E1 6AB, United Kingdom
www.pennedinthemargins.co.uk

All rights reserved

Introduction and selection © Tom Chivers & Martin Kratz

Copyright of the texts rests with the authors

The right of Tom Chivers and Martin Kratz to be identified as the editors of this work
has been asserted by them in accordance with Section 77 of the Copyright, Designs
and Patent Act 1988.

This book is in copyright. Subject to statutory exception and to provisions of relevant
collective licensing agreements, no reproduction of any part may take place without
the written permission of Penned in the Margins.

First published 2014

Printed and bound in the UK by Berforts Information Press Ltd

ISBN
978-1-908058-18-8

This book is sold subject to the condition that it shall not, by way of trade or otherwise,
be lent, re-sold, hired out, or otherwise circulated without the publisher's prior
consent in any form of binding or cover other than that in which it is published and
without a similar condition including this condition being imposed on the subsequent
purchaser.

Cover design by Ben Anslow
Map illustration by Nicholas Murray

CONTENTS

INTRODUCTION

Tom Chivers & Martin Kratz

THE 'REAL' MOUNT LONDON is situated somewhere on the boundary between British-Columbia and Alaska at a height of over 7,000 feet. Its moniker 'London' has nothing to do with the capital city of the United Kingdom, but is in honour of the American author Jack London. The 'virtual' Mount London, on the other hand, is the anthology of urban explorations which you are holding in your hands right now. It can be situated anywhere you like, and while its highest point is currently The Shard at just over 1,000 feet, collectively the elevations in this book are much higher — and who knows what monoliths the future holds. If Jack London's most famous novel is *The Call of the Wild*, then perhaps this book can be thought of as a call of the urban. Although it is none the less wild for it, with writers variously dangling from Battersea Power Station, woken by nocturnal blood sports, and on the brink of passing out with physical exertion.

    Mount London was conceived as a result of a conversation between the two of us, Martin and Tom; as an attempt to reimagine, and reconnect with, the physical topography of the city. Lest we forget, the earliest incarnation of London, as a Roman military settlement, was built across two small peaks — Cornhill and Ludgate Hill — and the freshwater stream that ran between them (the Walbrook). These gravel promontories would have provided strategic capabilities as they were easily defended and commanded a wide vista across the Thames, but they may also have assumed ritual significance. The seventeenth century antiquarian William

Camden believed that St Paul's Cathedral was built over the ruins of a temple to the Roman goddess Diana. In some cities, geography is felt as an imminent force — a haze in the peripheral vision, or a strain in the legs. Think Edinburgh or Rio de Janeiro, San Francisco, even Belfast. But it is almost inconceivable that the place we now call London — drained and levelled as it is, raised and filled out — was once an untamed environment of marshes and tidal creeks, forests, heathlands and hills.

It is *almost* inconceivable. Yet a recurring theme which the writers of *Mount London* touch on in their ascents is the way the bedrock of the city repeatedly bursts through its concrete crust, disturbing their experience of the built environment with its own underlying geology and history. Unlike Rome, a city famously built on seven hills, raising it from the marshes, London is thought more often in terms of its river. Capitoline, Palatine, Aventine, Caelian, Esquiline, Viminal and Quirinal seem to bear the full mythological weight of their city. Who in the same way would think of Stamford, Spring, Horsenden, Windmill, Snow, Forest or Lavender? At the same time, the explorations of urban elevations seem to be ghosted by their brothers and sisters from far-flung cities and terrains: The Shard mirroring the Burj Khalifa and advertised as a Shangri La; the Golgothan evocation of gibbets, gallows and bones; Babel in London's abundance of languages; Ararat in the recently flood-soaked landscape; and again and again in the building towards a shinier, taller, better city, the old idea of the New Jerusalem. And then, there are the mountains the writers themselves bring with them — from the Lakes and the Peaks, and from South Armagh.

As gridlocked as Everest (with Trafalgar Square its Hilary step?), London is neither *tabula rasa* nor virgin peak. There are many climbers currently dug in on its slopes, and many more who have come before. Wordsworth, the exemplary mountain poet, surveying the city from Westminster Bridge. The Sydenham Hill giant deep in foliage. Margaret Finch, Queen of the Gypsies, smoking her long pipe. Bunyan on his death bed in a Snow Hill pub. And who can forget: Doctor Who and the Cheetah People at the summit of Horsenden Hill. London's is a landscape dense with myths and the novice climber must be aware of their traces; free-climbing where possible, using the fixed ropes where they must.

Mount London, as we call it, is made up of seventeen hills, three towers, two heaths, one field, one mount, one very long staircase and one palace (which is, strictly speaking, a ridge with three peaks). Not one of them is high enough, by any official standards, to be deemed a mountain. But considered together, their accumulated altitude outstrips Ben Nevis by a good five hundred metres.

But what is a mountain without a mountaintop? What is an ascent without the crowning glory of reaching the summit, of planting your nation's flag? For every writer here who, on reaching the highest point, looks back across the city, discovers new, surprising vistas, there is another unsure they've even reached the top, confounded by its geography, who finds not peak but plateau, no hill but just a bump in the pavement.

The mountaineer is a kind of noble fool, always hanging from the precipice between bravery and recklessness. And like any true fool he not only play tricks on others, running the reader on fool's errands, but in turn is tricked himself:

> "What's that tiny thing that looks like St Paul's?" I said.
> It was St Paul's.

The figure of the hanged man is everywhere, swinging from the gibbet, but also the master of ropework, going where no one else can. The mountaineer, like the trickster, finds himself having it out repeatedly with his own body as he steels himself against the terrain. Many of the expeditions in this book reveal mountainous follies, their rubble strewn across the city from Northala Fields to Stave Hill to the ruins of the Crystal Palace. These buried, vestigial structures offer a counterpoint to the housing crisis that threatens to alter the dynamics of London forever, carving the landscape into *de facto* segregated zones for the rich.

One of the most striking results of the simple commission we gave to our contributors is the level of autobiography the idea of the mountain seemed to invite. Perhaps this impulse to measure ourselves, physically and mentally, against nature, is a hang-on from the Romantic poets. We might think of Wordsworth playing off the individual against the landscape in his poem 'Lines':

> Five years have past; five summers, with the length
> Of five long winters! and again I hear
> These waters, rolling from their mountain-springs
> With a soft inland murmur. — Once again
> Do I behold these steep and lofty cliffs,
> That on a wild secluded scene impress
> Thoughts of more deep seclusion; and connect
> The landscape with the quiet of the sky.

However, the deep sense of integration with nature which Wordsworth associates with his youth ('when like a roe / I bounded o'er the mountains by the sides / Of the deep rivers, and the lonely streams, / Wherever nature led') is replaced in much of the writing in *Mount London* by a palpable sense of tension. In some cases this tension carries an almost hostile sense of determination, which results in the idea of the mountain as something to be conquered. In other cases, we return to that sense of the mountain having its own agency, to be feared and respected. What is unique to the combination of mountain and city, however, is that image of the mountain forming the bedrock of the urban landscape, but also as an empty shape waiting to be filled by a rising skyline. In this sense, autobiographical reflections on the writer's past and present often find themselves negotiating with the future. While Wordsworth's poem also negotiates with the future, it is in a bid for posterity. The future in *Mount London* is something much more tenuous.

The twenty-five essays range from Stamford Hill in the north-east to Richmond Hill in the south-west, with clusters around Hampstead in the north and the corresponding south London ridge around Crystal Palace. Some will be familiar to all Londoners, others (such as Stave Hill and Horsenden Hill) tucked away in unfashionable suburbs. London is highest at its north-western edge, and if our selection appears to avoid this upland corner it is perhaps only in deference to Nick Papadimitriou, who has written so compellingly of the North Middlesex-South Hertfordshire Escarpment in his book *Scarp* (Sceptre, 2013).

This is not a guidebook. Nor is it a comprehensive index of the hills of London. Many of the city's most famous promontories — for instance, Primrose, Tower and Shooter's Hills — are absent. A larger project may even have included explorations of such vanished lumps and bumps as Tothill (Westminster) and the Whitechapel Mount. Our intention as editors is not encyclopedic but impressionistic: a partial selection of competing voices. We hope, above all, that by way of its gaps *Mount London* might inspire you to seek out summits of your own, to launch new ascents in a vertical city that just keeps on growing.

Tom Chivers & Martin Kratz
— April, 2014

MOUNT LONDON

The secret of the mountain is that the mountains simply exist, as
I do myself: the mountains exist simply, which I do not.

Peter Matthiessen, *The Snow Leopard*

Mount London
1,800m

16. *Battersea Power Station*
17. *Blackheath*
18. *Telegraph Hill*
19. *Lavender Hill*
20. *Denmark Hill*

21. *Richmond Hill*
22. *Brixton Hill*
23. *Forest Hill*
24. *Gipsy Hill*
25. *Crystal Palace*

STAMFORD HILL

Katy Evans-Bush

The Hill has always been there, of course. Rising above the surrounding everydayness, it raises its head and speaks to the other hills around it: Highgate, misty blue to the west in the evenings; Muswell Hill to the north; and Alexandra Park, where the Palace, with its glorious almost-modern transmitter, catches the sun's fire like a mirror and scatters it everywhere.

The Hill sees more with its all-seeing eye than the flat places below it, and its people pick up signals unavailable in the narrow Victorian canyons of Finsbury Park — whose name, *town of the fens*, tells you of its damp, low-lying nature — or Stoke Newington. Stamford Hill is the local apex: here the roads, the traffic, the human movement, have converged for two millennia and maybe more. The sky is huge. The light seems bigger than down below. It is said that when King James I was received here by the Mayor and aldermen on his first approach to London after ascending to the throne, he could see the whole of the city spread out before him.

One afternoon a tiny while ago, a ten-year-old girl was walking with her mum down an alleyway, a sort of narrow way, leading into Stoke Newington High Street. It was a nothing sort of early evening, and we were going from the friend's house where I had picked her up after work to, I imagine, the Turkish shop, and then home on the bus. Old houses (or cottages) alongside gave nothing away; there was a plant in a pot by a front door, there was a Victorian street lamp

— and ahead of them the main road teemed with the usual nonstop traffic: vans, cars, cyclists, and people from all over the globe.

We walked along, each with our bags and thoughts.

I said something: 'What do you want for supper?'

Or: 'So how was school?'

D said nothing, then shook her head and said:

'Oh! That was so *weird*.'

'What was?'

'Everything just disappeared', D said. 'Didn't you see it? It was all gone and it was olden days. The High Street was there, and it wasn't cars, it was ladies in long dresses and horses and carts.'

And then, just as fast as it went, it had all come tumbling back again, the buses and cyclists, the yummy mummies pushing over-designed buggies, the 20p guy, the off-duty journalists, the crazy Spanish kid with the guitar. The buildings, built in about the 1860s, had remained more or less the same. I asked a few more questions, and then we came out into the High Street itself.

Stoke Newington High Street, which momentarily disappeared on that day in around 2006, makes up a part of the Old North Road — what used to be called, in the very old days, Ermine Street, after the *Earningas*, a Saxon tribe in the fens — leaving the City at Bishopsgate and running in a straight-ish line all the way to Cambridge. It was a Roman Road, but the Roman name for it is forgotten. It crosses other Roman roads along its way — for instance, Old Street, which connects it to the far more ancient Watling Street (at one end, the scene of Boudicca's defeat; at the other, the route Chaucer's pilgrims and others followed from Southwark to Canterbury; and somewhere in the middle, the Old Kent Road, home of evangelical warehouse churches). About half a mile north of our disappearing act, when the road reaches the top of Stamford Hill — or Saundford or Sanford Hill, as it used to be known — it crosses another one, which led at one time down to the larger Saxon settlements by the River Lea, where King Alfred and the locals routed the Danes in a great battle. It now leads to Clapton Pond, where house prices are currently increasing out of all proportion to how *nice* the place actually is. (And after Clapton Pond you get to Sutton House, home of one of Thomas Cromwell's brightest henchmen. It still has its beautiful linenfold paneling, and its top floor is haunted by the ghost of a little dog.)

This road, we're saying, has seen a lot, over a lot of years. Even the Coach and Horses, which stands next to our mysterious narrow way and serves delicious Thai food in an old-fashioned-pub ambience, would have been there in whatever time my daughter tesseracted back to, because it was licensed in 1723. The village of Stoke Newington was spreading out from Church Street, filling out the landscape. There was so much traffic along this road that around 1715 several local parishes had petitioned Parliament for permission to erect toll gates, to raise the money to maintain it. There was a toll gate, or turnpike, in Kingsland to the south, and another on top of Stamford Hill, at the intersection of the two Roman roads.

Everyone passed along here: it was the north-south axis, a hive of enterprise, and also a portal to the green fields and farms beyond in rural Tottenham. You had farmers going to and from market, travellers to the north, and to the south, merchants and gentlemen and cobblers. Parties on their way to the pleasure gardens of the famous Mermaid Tavern in Mare Street. Students, kings and diplomats, highwaymen on their way to lie low in the provinces, brickmakers' carts, theatrical troupes, preachers.

In the 18th century Hackney was full of brickworks. The epicentre of industry was Hackney Wick, but at the top of Stamford Hill in 1694, one Francis Tyssen leased a property to a brickmaker called Ralph Harwood, and in 1721, 'One of several strips at Stamford Hill included a cottage, beside a length of nearly 150 feet, which was 'subleased to a Hoxton brickmaker''.[1]

This summit of Stamford Hill, where it crosses the old road to Clapton, forms — nowadays — a very large intersection with a tremendous sense of open space. It's this space you're invited to fill as you imagine the expanse of farms and fields stretching north to leafy Tottenham. Or as you think of the carts and carriages rumbling through the toll gate, or as you see in your mind's eye a gibbet, swinging in the gentle spring breezes of the 1740s with its Tyburn cargo, warning those travelling south to mind their manners while in the vicinity. (By the 1760s this gibbet had been moved to Upper Clapton, perhaps because by this stage there were some rather fine houses going up along the Hill itself, and it probably spoilt the view.)

It was suburban sprawl. It had been creeping up Church Street from Newington Green, and it had been creeping up from Hackney Wick, where the work and money and noise and mess were. And now it had reached to where (touch wood) even the hipsters of 2014 have not yet managed to penetrate: to the top of Stamford Hill. Hills are sacred and fortifying features: associated with mystical properties and faery doings, the sites of ancient rites and burials and sacrifices, stone circles and earthworks, towers and lookouts

---

[1] TFT Baker, *A History of the County of Middlesex, Vol 10: Newington and Stamford Hill,* 1995.

and hauntings. This one can be no different. It seems integral to its surroundings. Even the name 'Hackney', first mentioned in the 11th century, means 'raised place'.

So, standing on this highest point, let's pause and take in the fresh air. We're at a junction on whose corners stand, going clockwise from the northwest corner: an off-license and corner shop stuffed so full that the aisles are barely big enough to get through; Boots the Chemist, next to a bookies and Grodzinski's bakery; Barclay's bank in an Edwardian building, next to which the fine, three-storeyed, porticoed Cedar house once stood, leased to a brickmaker; and a Sainsbury's, cattycorner to the intersection the same way as the neighbourhood cinema was that stood there in the 1950s. In front of us flows the downward northern slope. We are with a Victorian gentleman, a classic of the type: an antiquarian and genealogist, contributor to the *Dictionary of National Biography*, compiler of *Men and Women of the Age*, and the man who wrote, in six volumes, a magnificent, anecdotal, exhaustive history of London's many parts: *Old and New London* (1878). His name is Edward Walford, and he had the advantage in life of having been educated (before matriculating at Oxford, of course) at the Church of England School in Hackney.

> On reaching the summit of the hill, where the two roads meet ... an entirely different scene presents itself, and we begin to feel that we have reached almost the limits of our journey in this direction. Green fields, trees, and hedge-rows now burst upon the view; and winding away to the north-east the road leads on towards the village of Tottenham, whither we will presently direct our steps.

> Before proceeding thither, however, we will give a glance back over

the ground we have wandered; and conjure up to our imagination the sweeping change which must have taken place within the last three or four centuries, when London was walled in on every side, and all away to the north was fields — "Moor Felde," "Smeeth Felde," and the like — and forest land, through which passed the lonely road, called "Hermen [or Ermine] Strete" ... after emerging from "Creple Gate," on its way by Stoke Newington, to St. Albans and the north. The swampy nature of the ground, too, in some parts is still indicated by the name of Finsbury (*Fensbury*); but all this, as we have seen, has long been built upon, and "Moorfields are fields no more."[2]

Our companion considers his short walk up from Stoke Newington itself:

Both sides of the road, as we pass up the hill, are occupied by rows of houses and detached villas, many of them of an elegant character, that almost force upon the recollection the lines of Cowper —

"Suburban villas, highway side retreats,
That dread th' encroachment of our growing streets.
Tight boxes, neatly sashed, and in a blaze
With all a July's sun's collected rays,
Delight the citizen, who, gasping there,
Breathes clouds of dust and calls it country air."[3]

The elegance and the villas took a while to materialise. In the 1760s there were a few merchants' houses beyond the turnpike, and some grander houses towards what is now upper Clapton — the Cedar House, for example. But most of the building was happening further

---

[2] Walford, Edward, *Old and New London*, Vol. 5, Chap. XLIV, 1878.
[3] Ibid.

to the south, in Stoke Newington Church Street on the one side, and around what was then known as Cockhanger Green (including a bowling green at its edges) on the other — beyond the Coach and Horses and Henry Sanford's brewery, and the little lane named after him, where my daughter saw the world disappear.

Aside from the brewers and brickmakers and merchants outside the gates, by the 1760s Stamford Hill was home to more than one distinguished Jewish family, including that of the Sephardic dynasty-founder Moses Vita Montefiore, who had come from Italy to take advantage of the relative liberalism of English laws. His grandson Abraham (who started life apprenticed to a Watling Street silk merchant called Mr Flower) married Henrietta Rothschild. Her brother, Nathan Mayer Rothschild, also built a house in Stamford Hill, just south of where we're standing. Nathan was one of five sons of another dynasty-founder, Amschel Rothschild. A colourful character, he started a textile company at twenty-one, before going into bullion. By 1818 he had amassed so much wealth that he was able to lend five million pounds to the Prussian government and enough gold to the Bank of England to ward off a liquidation crisis in the 1820s. He was a prominent figure in the movement to abolish slavery, and when Wellington defeated Napoleon at Waterloo, Nathan knew about it a day before the official messengers arrived.

Stamford Hill started getting built up around 1800, following the expansion of the 18th century in both Stoke Newington and Clapton. By the 1840s the wealthy families had begun to move further out — Nathan Mayer Rothschild went to Gunnersbury Park — and by the 1870s, as Edward Walford tells us, 'So much may the neighbourhood now be considered part of London, that the road itself is traversed by tram-cars, which run between the City and the top of Stamford Hill'. Indeed, we are standing with Mr Walford in front of two reasonable-sized tram shelters, which will definitely be present by 1882, and we may about to be run down by a double-decker steam conveyance.

But our genial guide Mr Walford vanishes; his day is over. The first synagogue opened in Stamford Hill in 1910. From 1926 the Haredim, or ultra-orthodox Jews, started to arrive. Now there are fifty synagogues, and if you look up Stamford Hill on Wikipedia the entire entry is about the Haredim. It is the third largest Haredi community in the world, and remains for the most part opaque.

I'm typing this on a Friday evening. The sun has just set and the light is soft, gold and purple, and the street is filled with amplified music to signal the beginning of Shabbat.

There is a sort of secret air, a secret time, another atmosphere, in this place which has been so heavily used for over two thousand years. In a house south-east of the summit of Stamford Hill, due south, perhaps, of the old Clapton gibbet; in a street that stems off the common where the Newingtonites of the late 18th century played bowls, where Henry Sanford had his brewery and built a row of Georgian townhouses that still stands; where the buses look almost the same as the trams did in 1889, where Marc Bolan grew up, where they stored all the uncollected rubbish during the great binmen's strike of 1979; in this house, full of an out-of-control energy, I would often wake in the night to swirling, or hovering, green shapes in the darkness of the bedroom. In this house, where my daughter was born, she used to wake up in the middle of the night all through her first eight years and see a box at the end of her bed. Sometimes she would sit up and try to reach this box, and when she reached out, it would disappear. She used to complain about it (and about her recurring nightmares about witches, so terrifying I never heard what happened in them). Later, when she was about eleven, I asked her what the box looked like. 'It was different every time', she said.

That was the house, built in 1865, where I woke up one night myself, and saw standing beside my bed a benign presence: a clear, green man, in sort of gelid outline; in middle age, not very tall, but portly; wearing what looked like 18th century Middle European clothing, including — as I realised later — a sort of fur-trimmed hat. He stood there. I opened and shut my eyes a few times, but he was still there. I couldn't tell if he knew I was there or not. So I settled down, shut my eyes, curled into the duvet and went back to sleep.

PARLIAMENT HILL

Helen Mort

I t's a daunting stretch of hill, cordoned on either side with orange tape. The strip of grass we stare down is wider than a road. Three hundred runners, crouched and ready. Skinny girls in garish vests: the orange of Hertfordshire, Derbyshire crimson. It seems like an eternity to wait in silence, but at last the gun pops and we surge forward up the incline. Not exactly as one, but less than the many we started as. Junior Girls. English Schools Championships. March 11th, 2000. My first real race.

There are elbows on all sides. The first 400 metres is about jockeying for position, finding your rhythm and your place in the pack, then settling for it. The risk is always in setting off too fast, exhausting yourself before the race has really got started. But when you're hemmed in by bodies, tripping over other people's feet, your instinct is to charge away. Got to keep this up for 3k, remember. I think about my coach, Tony, and what he'd say. *Keep them arms low. Stay relaxed.* I catch the chemical smell of Deep Heat and hear the crowd's shouts mingle to one roar. The Derbyshire pack has split up already. I'm dimly aware of a red vest somewhere in front and out to the right of me, but can't be sure. I can't really feel my legs yet, even though this first stretch is punishing, the incline slowing us all down.

We reach the top of the first hill and start to merge into a thinner stream of runners, about four or five deep. I glance over my shoulder. I'm a good way towards the back of the field. Rounding the corner is a shock: the ground drops away suddenly and surprises us, pulling us down, making our legs move faster than we'd like. Ahead, there's a muddy bend and it's pockmarked with single shoes, abandoned, sticking up out of the ground. The course gets churned up in places like this, corners where the water collects. Some of the front-runners must have had their spikes sucked clean from their feet. Instead of stopping, they've kept on running, not looking back. I imagine them surging round the next corner in bare feet, or incongruous in their socks. When I sink into the mud for a moment, it almost reaches my knees. We all goosestep our way through it, trying to move as quickly as we can. We look as if we're running in slow motion.

Time does strange things when you're racing. Fifteen minutes can last forever. There's a succession of endless rises and drops, artificial turns, patches of bald grass and swamps that sap us. And at every turn, there's a red-faced coach or team manager hollering at someone. *Come on Leoni, she's tiring. Keep it up, Bedfordshire. That's it Sarah, work through the field.* After a while, the sounds become bewildering. Any of them could be for you. My dad's somewhere out here. I wonder if he'll see me. There's always someone lying, yelling *not long now.* I look around again. I'm too far from the front to feel committed to giving it my all, but I'm far enough from the back not to worry about finishing anywhere near last. A girl in front is wheezing with effort, her breathing near hysterical. Just catch her up. Then focus on the next person's back and bobbing head. Pick them off now, one by one.

I was more on edge in the coach than I am here in the race. As the bus inched through the north of the city and the buildings got taller, denser, more stately, I'd felt my chest tighten. This was London. Most of us had never been before. When the coach swung through the gates towards Parliament Hill School and we saw all the other teams swarming round the buildings, an excited murmur ran through the bus. Kids who didn't know each other, united by the strangeness of the city. We'd come from Alfreton, Belper, Bolsover and Chesterfield. Places where the tallest buildings were the pub and the Jobcentre. Some of us were only twelve or thirteen. We felt like we'd been dropped here. But at the same time, Parliament Hill was just another taped-up course. It was no different from the playing fields at Shirebrook where we'd all qualified, months earlier, under the school sign from which someone had stolen the H, the E and the R, the wall where someone else had spraypainted 'shitebrook'. Every cross country course is the same.

Except it isn't. Those moments when your tunnel vision lifts, you think about where you are. Now, as the course takes us back on the long loop towards the finish, past some brief and leafless trees, I look down on all of London. Or what I guess is all of London. The tower blocks are jostling for position on the skyline. Some of them are like arms raised in class. The late winter air is making itself visible, white and cold. It looks a bit like the buildings have been breathing out and the sky's held each breath. There are buildings like pimples and buildings like pine cones. I try to imagine myself living in one of them. Even just being in one. I imagine myself in all of the cafes we passed on the bus, one by one, sitting with a thimble-sized coffee cup and a newspaper. Being an adult. If I was higher up, somewhere high in the air, I'd be able to see the arterial roads and the beetling cars, imagine the people moving through the streets of the city centre. I'd notice the green spaces and the tops of trees. But from here, the city's profile just interrupts the clouds. It gestures up to elsewhere as if that's all it needs to do.

I wonder what would happen if I took the brakes off, right here. If I let myself go, maybe I'd just keep on careering down into the city, down through Camden, through all the traffic lights, faster and faster into central London, like the painted eggs we lobbed down the hill a week earlier at school egg rolling. They went quicker and quicker until they smashed, or some just came to a rest in the longer grass at the bottom. Someone was a winner but I don't remember who. Some of the eggs bumped into each other and went off course. We are not high up for long enough to hold a thought. The course is flattening again now, leading us back towards the thing called the home straight. Although it isn't home, or straight. We all look like we're swimming through the mud now, moving our legs in slow motion. The field has thinned to something like single file. The tannoy booms out, announcing the names of the girls who have already crossed the line and won, far ahead of the rest of us. *Katrina Wootton, Bedfordshire. Emma Hunt, Bucks. Danielle Barnes, Devon.* I try to imagine being one of those girls. I wonder if it feels easier or harder running a race when you're winning it. I wonder if they've run here before. A girl in front of me slips and the mud takes her down. She's sliding on her front and other runners are hurdling her. We're all too selfish or too slow to gives her a hand up, but those are the rules. Everyone for themselves. It feels like London is above me now. I'm a foot sunk in the city's mud. I can't see the buildings, but I can feel them on every side. When the school comes back into view again, its windows stare us out.

In the last two hundred yards, the roar becomes overwhelming, no matter how far down the field you are. There are so many people leaning in on every side I feel dizzy. I don't know what they're saying or what they could be telling us to do now. My legs are heavy. My hair is plastered to my head. I'm carrying half of London on my feet.

When I cross the line, I can't stop.

HAMPSTEAD HEATH

SJ Fowler

not a sweet beast he is power
Jerome Rothenberg

I f it's only under very select environmental circumstances that
you may survive, then it's time to rethink your lifestyle. Because
surviving is the thing, and it isn't for certain that this will not be
tested, at some point. In fact, I'm being very gentle. It will be.

The monotonous roofs of the houses, tiled like beehives, the
mares in the pastures now drowned in the lido, the slow jogging pace
throws me into a vague gloom, that morose state of mind in which I
always approach the most successful realisation of my training ideas.
I can't really be bothered with this. I'm not going to Parliament Hill,
where all the recreational exercisers are. The only creative training
reality is what initially shocks our senses, and that which is not seen
until it is upon us. An enthusiast really sees only what he notices for
the first time or that he has to force himself to remember. Exercising
is and should be nothing else but a sensory revelation of the space
before us, for, if not that, it has hard justifications. Just in the viaduct
paddy, the cold water is very cold. Otherwise it is only the sticking
together and patching up of familiar and already fought fights, a
mere multiplying of what has already been seen, and experienced,
and so it is hard to do, again. The first incline begins to burn, the Hill
Garden, and this is the first point I think I should probably stop now,
I've done well enough doing this first hill and that might be enough,
it's been a nice day, no shame in stopping now, they have a nice cafe

here, could recline under the pagoda, do some writing, make notes for the essay on this run interspersed with sprints across the Heath for Tom, recover, maybe run back down, write that I did more hills, that that would be okay, no one would ever know, that I don't need to do another hill really, I did train yesterday, and the day before in fact, that is this my day off in fact, I deserve an easy day, that this one time it's fine to give in. It is surprising it hurts so grievously after the first. I keep running west, over the West Heath.

There is no appointment I fear more than hill sprints. I have been meeting them for nearly fifteen years, or half my life. And so I continue to attend, because of the value of that fear, I would imagine. I would use the word exercise in polite conversation, but with its connotation of recreation perhaps it is not the word most suited to the task of describing running up hills for no reason but the run itself. Or the hill itself. I have been conditioning for my entire conscious life. Often for competition. Training is the preparation of technique and the preparation of the mind for the experience of competition. Running up hills is part of the preparation of the body, to pre-figure possible machinic trauma to such an extent that it cannot become a factor in the application of technique, and thus leaving one free to apply technique, and also providing an essential sense of corporeal confidence in one's ability to not be hindered by physical limitations in its application. It is an act of scrupulous will, much akin to being frugal. This is how it began, anyway. This is how it was explained to me.

I had drunk my first beer with disgust (never again) and regretted smoking three cigarettes the evening before; and this child who played football, and tried to play wrestling, who was on the one hand still attached to the most childish things, and on the other torn by the most desperate viciousness, all of a sudden felt the fat, wet, sweating, burning sensation in his face. Both exhausted, because I had done my wind sprints the Sunday before, I was able to lift him from his feet, though he knew what was coming, though I telegraphed my shot in my dilapidated state. On my shoulders he didn't even reach out his arm to break the fall. I drove into his stomach as we landed, sweeping his legs across me, calculating, what acts of my mental and physical preparation had led to me slamming him, and he not slamming me. That accidental, thoughtless, harmless gesture remained with me as the most convulsive, passionate emotion of my whole childhood, that blotted out the psychological harm done by all else and others. I have four toes that do not retain much range of movement to this day. It is a normal, and accepted, part of the culture of wrestling to step on your opponent's toes in order to distract him to set up throws. A child's toes break easily.

Leg of mutton pond, dogs being walked. On Golders Hill, finding it easier than the last, though it is steeper. I try to not slow before I hit the incline, to accelerate into in fact, to sprint. I use the word sprint lightly. Within twenty metres it does not feel like a sprint, well not anymore. Rather a heavy jog, a desperate battle against lead weight. Never do I feel weightier, slower, less athletic, less mobile than on the last few paces of a hill sprint. I should be talking about the history of Hampstead Heath? I do care, but it doesn't feel possible, not being able to breathe unhindered. I have to take seated breaths at the top of the park, if I am to continue. Dogs investigate me. It is annoying when I am trying to focus on being resilient. A litany of animal tortures, I now wholeheartedly regret, and try to make amends for by being not only kind but mindful of all animals and the behaviour in me that serves them best, be it subservience, dominance or empathy. Humans are not afforded such a range of responsiveness. But then again I haven't done to humans what I've done to animals. I'm talking to myself already. Embarrassing to relate what slogans I speak to myself to keep on going. But I do, and that's actually all that matters. Up and east now, through Sandy Road to Sandy Heath, never ran there before, been told there are plenty of sharp inclines. Is scaling the hills of the Heath as satisfying as the lunchtime run from my work at the British Museum where, at median point, I touch the gaunt oak doors of St. Paul's Cathedral, and descend the steps where I spit? No, it feels like it lasts longer, and I have no special connection to this place. It is nice though. I'm not going to talk about its history, or its specific character, I've decided, because there are plenty of books on that and there is no way I will ever be able to live here.

Let's dispel the idiot's notion that people used to be stronger. Mentally tougher perhaps, and a wider range of stronger, but the strongest now are the strongest ever. Let's dispel the myth that exercise is somehow a purely modern phenomenon, an artifice of attaining physical strength. Since fighting began, training was. And there has always been fighting, lest you jellies forget. The only fabrication comes from those who exercise to look different, rather than to be physically and mentally stronger. Mysterious sacred objects which it was forbidden to touch. Such a desecration entailed a punishment which consisted of kneeling for hours behind the garage where it smelt of rats. Starting to retch on the Sandy Heath, it's clearly extremely off-putting for the joggers, who have never vomited because of exercise. They look at me with undisguised disdain. Some even with judgement, as though they are fitter than me. They haven't seen the many hills I've done before I enter their vision. The hills are not steep but multitudinous. There are no real views because I'm trying to stay conscious. A minute of rest, counting the seconds. Quite soft of me, but I feel much better.

A real circumstance born out of necessity is switched for a false circumstance of self-maintenance? Well first of all, as I've said, conditioning, or training, is as old as fighting, which along with procreating is one of *the things*. I can see Kenwood coming into view. There's that shitty lawn hill in front of the house at least. Second of all, staying strong when the world wants us to be weak is more real a choice than that of being strong or being dead. We have allowed physical weakness, that is the change, and all the better for that, I suppose, but that doesn't mean we should actively choose to be weak, as we do have a choice. Why does someone smoke? Why do they eat cheeseburgers and kebabs everyday? One hopes, I suppose, there will not be an epidemic or a mass flood, or some other apocalyptic event, but there is the temptation to will these things into being. Tourists taking pictures of me as I sprint the lawn in front of the house. They're likely here because part of Notting Hill was filmed here. Or because Marx liked to take his family here on days out. I veer towards the photographers, run past them as they look away and down. I'm heading downhill, perversely, into the woods. Have to avoid Parliament Hill, someone else is writing about that.

An assumption that manners are false, that they hide disingenuousness. But when chosen, when not mannerly or polite out of fear, weakness or choicelessness, manners are a profound human construct. Those who can bully those weaker than they and instead chose to seek out others as strong as they, in order to be challenged, to not be fearful, or slothful, well... why I am even writing about this? I'm at the ponds, up the incline before it bows out into the climb to Parliament Hill. The dry retch is in danger of becoming wet. I am more afraid now, now that it's coming to its end. I have only been out here for thirty minutes at most. Again, two people, sat on a blanket beneath a tree, are watching me. They are clearly cold. I am not cold.

The Heath carries with it the air of sex, but let's not dwell on it. Like where the horses trot, like fresh dung. I was told wearing two straps of your backpack signals your availability. The systemisation is appreciated. But not for me, the reading room, where I have worked for many years, treading boards, much more my dark corners. Underfurrows where even the cameras cannot catch sight of you, and so they are willing, when bored and feeling undervalued and low in esteem because of their boredom. Where Ezra Pound, Karl Marx, Oscar Wilde &c. I have dripped mine on the very much non-vegetal environmental. Hill sprints > testosterone, an increase in sexual desire? Not if you have cramps in your legs. How many old men are so disappointed in their hearts that it becomes so familiar to them and yet so strange, as if they had died sometime long ago and were faintly recognising the forgotten contours of dead things and events through a veil of incomprehension. Not much time to regret as I fatefully peter down the small incline to begin the last horrific stretch of sprinting back up towards Kenwood.

Unfortunately there does tend to be a causal relationship between how much an exercise hurts and how fit it makes you. Something about ascension at speed that takes perception beyond that basic meditative non-consciousness of long distance running, that will not allow you to place your mind elsewhere, far from the burning, and thrusts it absolutely into the moment of overwhelming pain, to concentrate it so intently that you do find yourself physiologically inured. The world changes on the final few sprints — beyond what you told yourself you'd be able to do, beyond any primary notion of physical limitation, when the legs are numb, the lungs heaving, when the euphoria of the calm that is coming soon seems so far away, when you most want to stop dead, and cannot do so because that feeling is so overwhelming to be obviously a false and soon shameful temptation. The world becomes new, colours actually change — the lack of oxygen getting to the brain blanches the world, bleaches it pale. I have sat down after a hill sprint and seen the world as entirely blue. Sound has changed, my ears are muffled and the chatter of the others on the hill, who ascended gently, is hollow and the other sounds, that were once in the background, come to the fore. It is both acute concentration and a transcendental, no-mind state. Whereas the pretence of a pure condition once willed me up the slopes, a lie I believed, now it is the reiteration of these simple and ineffable lessons. As blood roars through my body, muscle fibres tear, the respiratory system retches for air — the body is preparing to grow back stronger. So pliant is it, the thing that carries consciousness, so soft and weak, that it can be changed in such a short time, that thirty minutes on a hill, a tiny span of concentrated pain, when chosen, can set one ahead of hundreds of hours of suffering.

For comfort is not the benefit of Western civilisation. There is no comfort. A choice in the always painful process of growth is the great benefit of our transitory, wealthy world — that we now have a choice to choose the time and manner of our pain. Should we not do so, the very same mechanisms of that civilisation will most likely have us by their own ends, by the products, almost exclusive to them, of the very same industrial civilisation that provides such excess and such choice in the first place. Panting, hawking, seeing the Heath ponds as pure blue, unaware of my subjectivity but wholly being my physicality, on my knees, atop a hill, it is diabetes, heart disease, cancer and depression that seem such a long way away. They may happen anyway, but

I aim to run dogs down on the Heath, as I did once. Lots of dogs at Kenwood House. Though that dog I did make quit, it was old when exhausted in a heap and it was a half-dog, in mourning, and old, a domestic fashion dog. The others outran me so profoundly I am reminded how weak we are compared to the other apes and that helps me on, don't give up, keep going, my legs are gone from yesterday.

DARTMOUTH PARK HILL

Sarah Butler

And when they were up, they were up,
And when they were down, they were down,
And when they were only half-way up,
They were neither up nor down.
  The Grand Old Duke Of York

The French philosopher Michel de Certeau opens his essay 'Walking In The City' with a description of looking down on Manhattan from the 110th floor of the World Trade Centre: here we are at a distance, god-like voyeurs suddenly able to 'read' the 'text' of the 'bewitching world' of the city below.[1] The ordinary folk, however, live 'down below'. They both experience and create the city bodily by walking it (though here, de Certeau suggests, in the bustle and the chaos, they are unable to 'read' the text they create).

De Certeau's distinction between looking down from on high, and being down below, comes with the judgement that it is better to be in the midst of it all. *Down there* is reality, desire and truth; preferable to the arrogant voyeurism of the person on high, who believes they can look down on the city and understand it, and through that understanding seek to control it. I buy the politics of de Certeau's argument. I believe cities are made as much by the individual lives and stories of their inhabitants and visitors as they

---

[1]   De Certeau, M. (1988), Randall S. (trans.), *The Practice of Everyday Life*, Berkeley, University of California Press.

are by architectural plans and civil engineering. When I left London eight years after my reluctant arrival, I was leaving a city I adored, and adored because of exactly what de Certeau talks about — years of walking and cycling the streets, of getting involved in the messy, wonderful, constantly changing everydayness of the place. Yet, at the same time, I loved looking down on London. I spent years seeking out views of the city — from rooftops, windows, aeroplanes, from the summits of hills — endlessly delighted by the effect of looking at this place from different angles, and from on high.

I didn't want to move to London. I'm a Northerner, a Mancunian, used to easy access to the hills and mountains of the Peak District, Lake District, and Western Scotland. London, as far as I could tell, was a frenetic, expensive, aggressive city, best avoided. But circumstances conspired, and move I did, in the summer of 2004.

My then-partner and I rented a flat half way up Dartmouth Park Hill. It was — as the estate agent said, going to the very back of her folder of available properties — in need of modernisation. A slightly foreboding, detached house, with ineffective storage heaters, ugly textured wallpaper and an extraordinary lino kitchen floor.

I was in a city I didn't want to be in, in a weird, cold flat; but I had a view. The house was opposite a covered reservoir which opened up a vista east across London. A view even better at night than it was during the day — the distance jewelled and precious and the city somehow more straightforward.

Subsequently, I moved 'down' the Northern line — to Camden, Kennington, then Tooting Bec — joking to friends that I'd 'sunk' down to the bottom of London in search of affordable housing. In those early days, living on Dartmouth Park Hill, I'd often do a walk on the weekend that took in our nearby hills — Parliament Hill, Primrose Hill — I'd stand and look and I would always be struck by the fact that London stretched right out to the horizon and as far left and right as I could see. Do the equivalent in Manchester, and you can see where the city ends, the edges fading out into fields. London has no edges you can see, at least from any of the hills it offers.

I grew up in a family of walkers. We spent our weekends and holidays trekking up mountains for the pleasure of reaching the top and looking down at the world spread out below us — with all its beauty and colour, its strange patterns and shapes. As a newbie in London, the sense of elevation and space afforded by my first rented flat allowed me to feel some kind of ownership and control over a place I did not understand or particularly like. Does that make me an arrogant voyeur? Perhaps it does, but I needed it. As I whizzed downhill on my bike to cycle the canal network east to my job in Bethnal Green, as I embarked on the climb back home, feeling the gradient in my thighs, this odd flat, half-way up the hill, was a place I could stop and breathe and make sense of things.

Half-way up, or half-way down? Where we were felt like the top, because the road flattened out for a while before rising up again past Waterlow Park to Highgate Hill, but it was only half-way, a resting point. When I left the flat I could choose to go up or down; my decision established whether I was at the top or at the bottom in relation to that particular journey. I tend to think of hills as things to be climbed: the bottom is the beginning, the top is the end. But what if your starting point is elsewhere? What if you start at the top — as we start at the top of a page — and work your way downwards?

London's hills, at least around Dartmouth Park, are not linear. Top and bottom, beginning and end are not fixed or certain. It's not like walking up Snowden, or Scafell Pike, or Helvellyn. Dartmouth Park Hill 'ends' half way up Highgate Hill — its top is another's middle. And my flat was the summit of two other hills. Instead of going up to Highgate Hill or down to Tufnell Park Tube station, I could choose to walk east down Bickerton Road to buy pastries from the Jewish bakery in Archway, or west down Chester Road to eat pizza on Swain's Lane and then walk across the Heath. They might not be linear or easy to distinguish from each other, but these hills give dimension to the city; they allow us to feel the gradient of the earth in our muscles as we ascend or descend, to stop and look down on something bigger than the space we immediately inhabit. They constantly and subtly change our perspective.

Georges Perec, describing the act of writing, stated:

'Before, there was nothing, or almost nothing; afterwards, there isn't much, a few signs, but which are enough for there to be a top and a bottom, a beginning and an end, a right and a left, a recto and a verso'.[2]

Writing, then, as spatial: a physical process and object whose meaning is affected by its location in space (whether that be on the page or within the built environment) and which also *creates* space — a top and a bottom, a beginning and an end. For me, place and story, space and text are intimately and interestingly connected. The beginning, middle, end of a story / of a journey. The top, centre, bottom of a page / of a hill. How, then, might I *write* Dartmouth Park Hill?

---

[2]   Perec, G. (1997), 'Species of Spaces', *Species of Spaces and Other Pieces*, London: Penguin, 5-45.

Highgate Hill (more of a hill to climb)
                    Stressful junction (if you're cycling)
Road narrows
          and curves left
                    between park   and the church with the green roof
                              which I always notice
                                        when I'm walking on
                                        Hampstead Heath

Interesting concrete blocks of flats — balconies and sloped roofs
Weird pottery shop
          Traffic calming measures (various)

Turn-off towards Swain Lane and Hampstead Heath (west)
                              Turn-off towards Archway (east)

Our old flat   reservoir

          Lord Palmerston pub — purple paint, wooden floors —
                    where I met an old school friend for a drink
                    after years of not seeing him.

          That flat we looked at buying but didn't.

                    School — dark concrete, tall fence
          Hairdressers — nice green paint

          GP with tweed jacket who gave
          me a flu jab without asking first and
          sent me elsewhere to get a smear test.

          Dodgy Irish pub/nightclub (never went in)
          Italian restaurant I always meant to go to but never did.
          Tufnell Park Tube

That's my Dartmouth Park Hill, climbing up, sinking down the page. It is more populated, more personal, between my old flat and Tufnell Park Tube because that's the route I took most often, into the 'down below' of London. Writers often talk about having a sense of being always, slightly on the outside of things. They talk about the need to both live in and engage with the world and at the same time hold back, in order to observe and understand and express something about what they see (and, yes, perhaps, to try and exert some sort of order and control).

Maybe that's why being half-way up, half-way down, neither up nor down, suited me so well. Dartmouth Park Hill offered a structure to read the city. It gave me a sense — however ambiguous and changeable — of a bottom, a middle and a top. It gave me a view, however messy and uncontained, of other parts of London. It gave me somewhere to stop and catch my breath.

HAMPSTEAD UNDERGROUND STATION EMERGENCY STAIRCASE

Martin Kratz

The terms *geophony*, *biophony* and *anthrophony* were coined by the bioacoustician Bernie Krause to divide a soundscape into three sources: sounds of the earth, sounds of the animals and plants, and human sounds.[1] The undifferentiated barrage of sound one is assaulted with when disembarking the train in an underground station can helpfully be thought of in these same terms.

The anthrophonic sounds are the most diverse and immediately obvious: they include both the sounds of conversations between commuters, tannoy speaker announcements, the rustle of clothes, the varying sounds of rubber or leather tread on the concrete, as well as the bleeps of digital signaling devices, the hiss of compressed air, the draw of ventilation shafts, lift mechanics, and the full gamut of noise clattered into the atmosphere by the rolling stock one leaves behind on the way to the surface.

Biophonic sounds are conspicuous by their absence. (During a particularly emphatic lull in the traffic one *might* catch the panicked beat of pigeon wings scouring for an exit to ascend out of, or imagine the skittering of rats). The geophony is surprising in the sense that despite being this deep underground, one hears no raw earth sounds, no suckling of quicksand, no terrifying rush of landslips. Instead,

---

[1] Bernie Krause, *The Great Animal Orchestra: Finding the Origins of Music in the World's Wild Places* (London: Profile Books, 2012).

one's ears are insistently buffeted by the wind in the bends of the corridors, its pitch modulated and amplified by the vast resonating chamber of the London Underground system.

The effect on the ear, as these sounds clamour for one's attention is jarring. The effect of 'jarring' by underground machinery is also precisely what nineteenth century Hampstead residents feared would lead to the destruction of Hampstead Heath's surface-ecosystem, as tree roots lost purchase on the loosened soil.[2] These fears were unfounded. What made the excavation of this branch of the Northern Line significantly different from others was precisely 'its depth below ground in places because of the rising country through which it ran'. The deepest point of the line is approximately 250 feet, packed safely in London Clay like a kidney in suet. This point lies several hundred yards north of Hampstead Station, placing it somewhere along Heath Street, which was also to be the station's original name. The station itself is 192 feet deep, and as well as having the deepest lift shaft on the Underground, it has an emergency staircase with over 320 steps.[3]

The Staircase in the Hill. While the ascent out of the underground inevitably invokes a sense of the Orphic, the containing interiority of the hill (and the presence of rats) feels much more Pied Piper of Hamelin, or Peter Pan's Lost Boys, or Blake's 'The Chimney Sweeper'. It also invokes a series of modern mythologies, from Neil Gaiman's

---

[2] Christian Wolmar, *The Subterranean Railway: How the London Underground Was Built & How it Changed the City Forever* (London: Atlantic Books, 2004).

[3] John R. Day, *The Story of London's Underground: A London Transport Publication* (London: London Transport, 1963).

Down Street in his alternative vision of London, *Neverwhere*, to Gollum's grotto. The geophonic whistle of subterranean wind in particular, split on tunnel corners, roughed up on edges of tiles and their strike-board grouting, resonates with Tolkien's decision to inflect Gollum's voice with its trademark sibilance. From every dark corner, it hisses: *My precioussss…*

The visual noise also jars: from London Underground's ubiquitous roundel to posters for perfume, all amplified by the harsh electric lighting. The emergency staircase sign marks the point at which two different ascents become possible: the effortless journey in a high-speed elevator or the trudge up the long and winding stairs. In fact, the journey by lift is not entirely effortless as there is a strong chance of having to queue. But nobody takes the stairs. The sign warns them off:

> This stairway
> has over
> 320 steps
>
> Do not use
> except in
> emergency

It could be some sort of poem. The first two lines of each stanza contain three syllables each. The complete syllabic count reads 3/3/7 and 3/3/4. The full-length of the number of steps (the full scale of the ascent) and the way it exceeds the poem is betrayed by the fact that it is represented numerically, rather than reading as follows:

> This stairway
> has over

three hundred and twenty steps

Do not use
except in
emergency

The missing punctuation compounds the sign's threatening imperative. *Go this way*, it says, *and things go missing. I lost my punctuation. You might lose your head.* Hampstead has a history of catalexis or headlessness. In the early days of the Charing Cross, Euston & Hampstead Railway, the station witnessed an anthrophonic decapitation of the station's own name:

> Another source of complaint was the poor accent of the gatemen who, despite the nameplates and differently coloured tiles at each stop, were required to shout the name of every station, turning Tottenham Court Road into *Totnacorranex*, Hampstead into *Ampstid* and Highgate into *Iggit*.[4]

Recording the ascent from the station platform, past the sign and up the stairs with a microphone, the sound of voices and immediate platform noises drop away very rapidly, until for the greater part of the recording all one can hear is the sound of feet slapping stone on stone on stone over 320 times. There is little variation. Even the wind starts to drop. The footsteps become so monotonous, that in a recording of no more than 4 min 9s, the effect of their repetition morphs the sound into a giant tap dripping. The aural tedium of light wind and heavy footsteps is in fact interrupted only once, by the gurgle of water in a cooling duct. A cooling duct or a similar piece

---

[4] Wolmar.

of infrastructure. Like one's own intestines, while the mechanical outcome of the Underground's machinery is evident, one does not recognize every component that facilitates it, or know its name or its exact purpose.

A CCTV camera is mounted in the same place on every stair loop. Coupled with the warning of the sign, a certain anxiety pervades the mood in the stairwell. There is a sense of speeding up at the points where one is being watched. This is how a camera, a visual tool, can slow and accelerated the rhythms of a city. However, balanced out by the increasing exertion the stairs demand, the pace of the footsteps on the recording remains constant. Only one's laboured breathing indicates the exhaustion that begins to set in.

Not exhaustion. Expiration. As one rises, and the monotony and increasing exertion set in, the stairwell fills with more myths: *The Fall of the House of Usher*, Antigone buried alive in her cave in the hillside, the Morlocks. The myths are accompanied by their counterforce, the desire to be released from the city's enclosing darkness:

> And by came an Angel who had a bright key,
> And he opened the coffins & set them all free

In 1912, the debut poster by Underground and London Transport artist Walter E. Spradbery depicted a pastoral scene from Hampstead Heath. An avenue of English trees variously filters the sun into shades of gold and hazel. A woman in a white dress peeks out from behind one of the trees' deep trunks, carrying a bright read parasol. She is the only person in the picture, free to shine, no longer eclipsed by the occluding inner city throng. The poster reads:

FOR HAMPSTEAD HEATH
CLAIM YOUR PLACE
    IN THE SUN
BOOK TO GOLDER'S GREEN
    OR HAMPSTEAD[5]

The lines 'Claim your place | in the sun' are written in red. The text around them is written in white. The poster was used five years after the station opened, enticing people into the suburbs.The 'countryside' no further than a hop and a skip away.

And claiming one's place in the sun quickly develops into the climber's own primary desire. Towards the top of the stairs, it becomes apparent how considerable the rise in the land here really is. The only indication that one is approaching the exit is the growing leg pain and chest pain. Suddenly, there is a subtle change in the air, to which the climber otherwise stultified by the climb's monotony is instantly sensitive. Then a gradual increase in anthrophonic activity. The guards and commuters are muttering to each other. The shocking piston-shunt of the barriers echoes down the hall. The barrier's bleep accepts and declines Oyster cards. The traffic of cars arrives from outside. The wind picks up. The sunlight forces you to squint like a mole. You are a mole. You were never a climber. You were always a digger. You haven't made a mountain out of a molehill. A molehill *is* a mountain.

---

[5]   Jonathan Riddell, *Pleasure Trips by Underground* (Middlesex: Capital Transport Publishing, 1998).

SPRING HILL

Gareth E. Rees

I prepare for my ascent up the north-eastern ridge of Clapton with a pint of hoppy ale in a pub by the Lea Bridge Roundabout. My destination is the dark side of Hackney's moon: Springfield Park, an exposed outcrop of gravels laid down by the swollen meltwaters of that Anglian glaciation which sculpted the modern Lea Valley. Its sheer slope faces away from urbanised Hackney, overlooking cormorant-infested reservoirs, industrial estates and ancient marshland.

Since the gravels were first laid down, this elevation has exerted a gravitational pull on settlers. Until the 18th century, Clapton was known as Clopton, the 'farm on the hill', from the Old English word for farm: *clop*. The road leading from the village of Hackney towards this hill was called Hackney Lane. Today, it's a traffic-heavy artery known as Lower Clapton Road, Upper Clapton Road and, at its apex, Clapton Common. It draws me northwards from the pub through a clamour of bus gears, past The Crooked Billet — newly gentrified, gunship grey — toward Betfred, Tesco and noisy hair salons. Some of the shop fronts are retarded in time: orange launderette with 1970s frontage; L. Ives and Sons Ltd, long-closed, thick with cowbwebs, like a tomb behind glass. Neighbouring Metro Retro is a faux throwback, with its hippy floral dresses and tweed.

The road steepens through a parade of eateries: Hot Pot Caribbean, King Fried Chicken, Anatolia kebab joint, Sodo Pizza, Fisherman's Inn chip shop, Wu Chinese. These are the restaurants of outpost towns in mountain ranges, where travellers gorge on carbs before a trek. Fish stare from a bed of ice outside Elif Express, where walls of fruit 'n' veg soak up the car fumes. Fridges spill onto the street from a domestic appliance store. Outside a money transfer shop, a hooded man dances from foot to foot, jabbering frantically at a middle-aged bloke in a flat cap.

From there, the Shell station, a last chance to fill up. Across the road a kosher butcher marks the transition from a predominantly Caribbean and Polish community to a Haredi one. The shop is sparse, an empty shopping trolley in the window. A few doors up is Klein's mini market, bustling with women in headscarves. Finally Ashburn Glazing, another Jewish business. Then I'm above the cloud line. The slope flattens out, the atmosphere thins. Shops give way to blocks of flats — the Northwold and Wigan Estates — and 1930s houses with bay windows bearing CCTV warnings. Postmen weave through gates. An old lady pulls her shopping hoard in a quilted trolley. A bearded man strides by in leather jacket, sockless, with rolled up tracksuit bottoms. Haredi children pour from a Victorian end-terrace house, next to a decayed, flaking façade which bears the sign *New Springfield Hotel*. The memory of that earlier hill climb fades fast. There's no up or down, no east or west, only rows of houses flanking a stream of slow-moving single lane traffic. Suddenly I lose all sense of topography. This is easy to do in London. The city is a concrete platform laid upon a wild landscape of marshes, rivers, terraces, gravels and clay, cluttered with rhino bones and Neanderthal skulls. Walking the streets, it's easy to forget what lies beneath. But here suddenly is a sign on the pavement which points east, bearing the words 'Springfield' and 'capital ring'. Fail to notice this and you would move on, oblivious, to the pleasant green of

Clapton Common. You'd never realise you were so close to the edge of a geological precipice. Not unless, like me, you turn from the road and hurry between the Springfield Court and Keir Hardie estates through the gates of a park, past a pond where moorhens and ducks circle a spurting water feature.

Suddenly London drops away and the sky opens up to the universe. I stand at the edge of a gigantic crack in the city. From the ridge of a steep slope known as Wilson's Hill I look out over a valley of meadows, sparkling reservoirs and marshland, striated with overhead train lines. Pylons stride over ramshackle warehouse roofs and gas cylinders. A cloud shadow darkens a sea of wild grass, where cows graze beside a Victorian railway bridge. On distant hills slate roofs and window panes glisten in a shroud of rain. They seem to be from another time, another city, another country. At one time this was literally true. The Lea River snaking through the valley below formed The Danelaw, the border between Saxon England and Danish Viking territory. From this spot a Saxon warrior would have been able to see the fires of his enemy burning. Today isolated figures move through the terrain like ghosts. Dog walkers, blackberry pickers, kissing couples, junkies, drinkers, hedonists out seeking pleasures. Sometimes on a Sunday morning you can hear the dying heartbeat of a rave behind the railway lines.

In 1908, the authors Walter Besant and G.E. Mitton wrote an account of a journey through Hackney and Stoke Newington. They say of this place: 'We feel we have got to the edge of the world or, at any rate, to the extreme edge of London as we stand on the broken heights of green grass and see the sudden drop in the ground which runs away to the stealthily flowing river, and beyond it again the shimmering sheets of water belonging to one of the great water companies, edged with stiff Lombardy poplars.'

This 'broken height' has always been the *summa cavea* of the Lea Valley's amphitheatre. The ridge on which I stand is lined with manicured rectangular hedges which cradle viewing benches. From this vantage point you can see London's history strewn in fragments across a deep green bowl: an old copper mill, the ossified spine of a dead aqueduct behind the medieval grazing meadows known as Lammas Land. Geese flock over a Victorian railway bridge on Walthamstow marsh where the first British aeroplane was built and flown in 1909, and guns rattled at the Luftwaffe from trenches during the Blitz. Look harder and you can peer even deeper into the chasm of time. In allotments by the river, a woman digs trenches for potatoes. Boat dwellers burn wood fires. Travellers pick wild flowers. A kestrel hovers over the rushes. A long-horned cow flicks away a wasp with its tail. These are remnants of that world which existed when Clapton was the Farm on the Hill. Their persistence is a phenomenon. A relentlessly expanding London has covered much of the countryside in a concrete glacier, grinding its topographical features beneath the weight of time. Yet here is a rare place where geology is exposed, nature flourishes, and the streets boast of their acclivity: Spring Hill, Baker's Hill, Big Hill, Mount Pleasant Lane, High Hill Ferry. It is not their height above sea level which is remarkable — there are many higher spots in London — but their steepness in relation to the flood-plain. Like Hackney itself this place is defined by its relation to the marshes.

Hackney was first recorded as a name in 1198. It comes from the Saxon 'Haca's ey' which means 'raised ground in marshland' (*ey*) owned by a Dane mostly likely named Haca or Hacon. It was formed by gravel deposits from swollen waters in the glacial aftermath. Springfield Park is an outcrop of such gravels, overlaid with brick earth, which sits on upon a layer of London clay. When water filters down through these gravels it hits the impervious clay and seeps out as springs. It was these well-watered gravels which enticed early settlers. Flints, a Palaeolithic axe and Roman artefacts have been found in the park. Also: coffins, human bones and a Saxon boat. According to Mitton, on these heights 'may have stood a Roman villa part dwelling and part fortress or watch-tower and the residence of the military commandant of this prominent and, therefore, important outpost of Roman London.'

In medieval times the hill was rural and remained so until the late 18th century, when they began to extract the brick earth for the construction of that city which was spreading out towards villages and farmlands, hungry for materials. Some of it was turned into bricks for three houses built on the land: the Chestnuts, Spring House and Springfield House. Only the last remains today, now a cafeteria known as the White Lodge.

In the 1820s the point on the riverside below Springfield Park, known as High Hill Ferry, became populated by workers serving a booming local leisure industry. This area of Clapton was known as a 'veritable Alsatia', a sanctuary separated from the grind of the industrialising city. Until the early 20th century pleasure-seekers came from the grubbier parts of London to holiday by the river, frolicking beneath the poplars and drinking in one of the three busy pubs: The Robin Hood, The Beehive and the Anchor and Hope. Visitors took romantic strolls up the heights of Springfield, considered at that time to be the equal of Richmond Hill. At the summit are two old beech trees, every inch of their bark scarred with initials, a living palimpsest bearing successive declarations of love. A poem by local Sarah Couch about the two beeches, pinned to the notice-board in the White Lodge, reads: 'they knew Queen Victoria, they stood through storms and hurricane, and still they smile on Springfield, they beam across the marshes, they smile on you and me'. While lovers gazed out from beneath these trees, they might have noticed the rustling of bushes in the valley below, from those who sought the more illicit pleasures offered by the marshes for city folk seeking refuge from prying eyes. As the old music hall song goes: 'One day over the Lea my boyfriend did it to me, he did it once, he did it twice, then he had the cheek to say it weren't nice.'

Eventually, the days of Hackney's Riviera came to an end. The waterfront became lined with warehouses and timber yards. During the Blitz the marshes were enlisted for the war effort, hosting anti-aircraft guns. Bombs pounded to hell the houses around the Anchor and Hope. After the war, deprivation and industrial decline blighted Hackney. By the late 1990s the old rural ascent that was once Hackney Lane became known as Murder Mile. The idea of holiday-makers flocking to Clapton would have seemed a joke, such was its reputation. For many Londoners, Clapton wasn't even worth going to for a pint. But in the wake of Hackney's recent gentrification, the slopes of Springfield have become once again a veritable Alsatia, for those initiated in its magic.

As I look down from atop Wilson's Hill I see tennis players on the courts, children clambering on a wooden boat in the playground and a woman doing Tai Chi beneath a tree. Two runners puff up the slope. An elderly man meditates in the uncultivated grass. A Haredi man smoking a cigarette blethers on his mobile phone by the bandstand. He's one of the many who come here to talk freely, away from eager ears. Giggling drifts from the hedges where the viewing benches are concealed. A solitary drinker crushes a Special Brew can beneath his heel. A toddler chases a duck, laughing. Coils of smoke rise from the marina below. People are chattering at café tables outside the White Lodge. I smell lunch.

It's when snow comes to London that Springfield reveals its enduring gravity. Children have a keen instinct for sniffing out treasures in a city's topography: those nooks, dens and secret woods; places for play. As Hackney turns white, they come walking towards the hill from all directions, dragging sledges, bin liners, old scraps of plastic. They begin to slide screaming down the hill, one after another, turning a strip of grass into a black ice runway. Up they walk, down they slide. Even when the snow melts and the black ice becomes a chute of mud, they carry on regardless, eking out every last drop of pleasure, faces slathered in raw earth. It's hard to blame them. In the East End of London, people crave height. Some for the brief feeling of liberty which comes with seeing far out into the distance, so unusual in a claustrophobic world of Victorian terraces, Brutalist estates and tower blocks. For others, it's not the height but the falling from that height which is the pleasure. The letting go.

After I've stood long enough at the pinnacle of my ascent up Springfield, I know in my heart that it's time to go. I take one last look at the procession of pylons marching through the reservoirs towards a distant England. Behind me, geese are assembled by the pond, ready to launch across the wide open East.

HORSENDEN HILL

Justin Hopper

T his was the kind of fog that no winter's sun could burn. Thick, musty, a mist that usually rolls in off the coast as a warning; a Lovecraftian fog. Plodding figures came through it, vague outlines at first: a six-legged beast, lurching forward? No, a woman leaning into her pram. A man with a double-fisted claw? No, a shopkeeper rifling through his key ring. Two-headed monster, chimeric and lunging? No, a tiny woman being walked by her hound.

Even the broad dullness of the suburbs is given a taste of the weird when swaddled in such mist — and on first encounter, Perivale, West London, has few rivals when it comes to "broad" and "dull". A mere twenty minutes on the Central Line from the West End, Perivale feels of a different era, as though it may still harbor trainspotters and show the Open University all day. And yet as I push north through the fog along Horsenden Lane, the suburban cryptozoology tapers to emptiness. The few souls appearing near the Tube station peter out, and the shopkeepers' housing estates give way to the silent Saxon slopes of Horsenden Hill.

Despite their static nature, we often assign anthropomorphic duties to the hills that inhabit or ring our cities. Some urban hills nestle beside us or cradle us in their arms; others tower above us with an indifferent shrug, or lift us on their magnanimous shoulders. Appropriately for its Ealing neighbourhood, Horsenden Hill sprawls. It creeps from a wide base to its still-broad peak eighty-five metres above sea level, almost unnoticed beside the also-creeping housing plots and corner shops of Sudbury, Perivale and Greenford. The sprawl and creep of our suburbs is double-edged — part insidious blandness, part postmodern eerie (think Stepford and Midwich). And so, too, with Horsenden Hill. Because, for all the taming of its suburban yoke, just beneath this waxed veneer Horsenden is a wilderness.

A few minutes walk north of Perivale Tube station, I came to a small park spiked off on the west side of the road. Empty on a foggy weekday morning, a chalked-up pavement told of recent playground escapades: Alfa, Nimka and Twist competing in some no-doubt complicated series of events. (Going by the coloured-in gold and purple stars, I'd back Alfa, if Ladbrokes is still taking.) Peeking through the mist were swings and carousels, empty, begging for a soundtrack of sourceless whistling or Theremin. And in the center of it all, a small, nonchalant stone circle — we'll call it Parkhenge, or Playbury — comprised of a dozen toddler-sized faux-Sarsens.

To some, Playbury might be something of an inside joke, marking the space between the Health and Safety suburban plains and Horsenden Hill's geography of Iron Age fort and Saxon myth. Just beyond the park, the Capital Ring footpath — and the Grand Union Canal that it follows — acts as one of London's many boundaries between city and beyond. On the other side of the canal, just past the fences woven from thorny stalks by tenants of the houseboat moorings, Horsenden Hill begins its stealthy re-wilding.

A few brief centuries ago Horsenden Hill and its surroundings for miles in every direction were covered in forest. 'Densely-wooded thickets,' according to one chronicler, thundering with stag and boar. As recently as the turn of the last century the area's farmlands were punctuated with thick woods; the nearby agro-businesses of Greenford were still the exception to the rule by the time of the Great War.

Past the canal and the extant buildings of Horsenden Farm, now operated part-time by the Countryside Stewardship Scheme, I picked my way through an overgrown deadwood pile, left to encourage the insect population. A few steps further north, up Horsenden's subtle slope (and past the requisite car park), the focused tree line blurred into woods. Here, at the insect dwelling, stood an outbuilding entirely covered with sprawling weeds, stacks of wood and dewy leaves, seasonally devoid of even their crawling inhabitants. This was nothing like that forest of legend, but offered a glimpse of what might be. Perhaps, given not centuries but merely a few decades, Horsenden Hill could regain its natural state. On the west side of the hill stood proof that this was, indeed, the way things might go.

Walking between the remains of the old Ballot Box pub and the scattered houses of the tiny hamlet of Brabsden Green isn't as simple as it sounds, particularly on a wet autumn's morning. Holding on to a tree branch, I would perch my foot on a twisted bit of old iron or the ramshackle stones of a former retaining wall and lean forward into the thicket. A few hundred metres south of the Ballot Box's current location, these few crumbling stones are all that remain of Brabsden Green, its shin-high well-stones periscoping from beneath the brambles. Yet the last vestiges of the village, which once boasted a dozen cottages, a few grand houses, a church and a shop, fell under the wrecking ball not centuries hence, but within my own lifetime.

You'd likely miss Brabsden Green were it not for the Ealing Council historical marker at the site of the old Ballot Box. (Amongst other things, this board explains the origins of the pub's name: it served as the voting place for workers on the canal.) Photographs on the marker show the latter days of Brabsden Green, but try as I might, I couldn't map these Victorian village structures onto the wild oblivion before me. There was a botanical dissonance for certain — overgrown privet and feral bay trees stood out, like the splash on a wall that's been whitewashed of graffiti. But even walking along the retaining wall that forms the most definitive part of old Brabsden Green, it felt almost impossible that, forty years ago, people still lived here; that within living memory the mottled forest floor on which I stood, a stone's throw from London's rails, was a pub.

In the early 19th century, Brabsden Green was bustling but poor. When the nearby common land was enclosed, part of Brabsden's productive land was deemed "Poor's Land", its rents given to buy fuel for the locals who once gleaned theirs from that village green. On an 1865 OS map, Brabsden is flourishing; within forty years that fuel-land is one man's own, a grand, doomed oriental-style house owned by an aged Imperial veteran. Another generation and the trees, patiently waiting, had retaken Brabsden, inch-by-inch.

A short scramble from Brabsden Green, up the steeper side of the hill, and I was alone — completely alone — at the top of Horsenden Hill. The thicket of Brabsden's roadside wood long behind, this is a bald, modern spot, surrounded by golf courses. The current Ballot Box pub, just north of the Hill, fits right in: it's warehouse-sized before you even consider the car park and kids' area. And yet, on a misty morning, alone at Horsenden's flat summit, it's not difficult to imagine why iron-age settlers first sought safety on the mount.

The Victorian antiquarian Sir Montagu Sharpe posits Horsenden Hill as one of the natural alignment of hills used to guide ancient Britons through the dense 'primeval' Middlesex forest — and the fort ('don') at 'Horsa-don' as part of the defenses from which they raided Roman invaders. (Horsenden Lane — the road, running West of the Hill, on which Brabsden Green once thrived — is that same millennia-old track.) On a clear day, with the right mindset, these trackways become apparent — erase the lines of beige rooftops and antennae and, for twenty-five miles in any direction, the hills arise.

At least one version of local legend gives us a champion of the suburban wild. King Horsa had a bright and beautiful daughter named Ealine (Ealing) who, through the tragedies of tribal politics, married an ignorant dolt. Fortunately, Ealine also had a starling she'd taught to speak, which she used to send word to her father that she wanted a Saxon-style divorce. The armies of Horsa and his dumb-but-strong son-in-law Bren met on the battlefield, and Horsa, while victorious, was mortally wounded. Ealine and the King's forces buried Horsa and his warhorse in the mound that now caps Horsenden Hill.

'Even now,' quotes one Victorian chronicle, 'the affrighted peasant, as he hastily passes round the brow of the hill at the witching hour of night, fancies he hears the solemn tread of Horsa's giant steed as he paces round the place of his sepulture; and some go so far as to affirm they have seen the shadowy form of the dead warrior when the pale moon illumines the hill, and the white mists curl upwards from the vale at its foot.'

I scrambled back down steps cut into the hillside, from which I could hear children playing — schoolyard antics no doubt hampered by high-vis vests and adequate supervision. Perhaps Alfa, Nimka and Twist were involved in a rematch. But under the circumstances — the sun jutting out, yet somehow not burning away a puff of the mist — it rang directionless and unknown; overtones of Midwich, of Hanging Rock and, most of all, of Ace and the hunt.

In what is possibly Horsenden Hill's only encounter with pop culture, the final storyline of the long original run of *Doctor Who* was set, and filmed, in Perivale and on the Hill. Appropriately, it's titled *Survival*. Horsenden Hill plays multiple roles: as itself, as an alien planet populated by the hunter-gatherer Cheetah People, and as a stand-in for the primeval wilderness that humanity has suppressed but never wholly forgotten.

Shot towards the end of Thatcher's reign, *Survival* is about everything one might expect of that era: individualism and communal struggle, social Darwinism, suburban boredom and suburban fear. Kids are disappearing from Perivale, the hometown of The Doctor's companion in time travel, Ace. It turns out these teens are being transported to a strange planet where the once-intelligent Cheetah People have de-evolved and now hunt humans for sport.

Horsenden Hill plays its roles magnificently. As stoically as it embodies the bored suburban teens' refuge, a spot for covert Saturday night drinking sessions and Sunday afternoon fitness clubs alike, the Hill also diligently manifests as wilderness, like it could swallow you up at will. The storyline's final battle is fought upon Horsenden Hill's flat mount, the future of all humanity hanging in the balance: civilization or 'the wild'?

'The affrighted peasant ... fancies he hears the solemn tread of Horsa's giant steed.'

We sometimes forget that this landscape is a tenuous one, that the picturesque manicure of our hillsides and our steeple-spiked urban frameworks are, in many ways, future ruins. But mountaintops give us a view that transcends mere miles. The beetles of Horsenden Farm's deadwood piles reminded me of a term from entomology: montane (mountain-based) ecologies are entirely separate from those of the surrounding terrain. So montane ecologies throw up unique, almost Galapagan species — once-familiar beasts can appear in their mists with six legs, two heads, or claws. To insects, mountains might as well be islands. And from our urban montane regions we can, likewise, view the city not as linear terrain, but as an archipelago: church spires and shopping blocks connected by thin bridges of canal and rail lines, otherwise swallowed by oceanic housing.

Walking, listening, waiting at the top of Horsenden Hill, I could see its surroundings with such montane vantage, and could colour these beiges and stone-greys a shade of Brabsden Green. In his 19th century apocalyptic novel *After London* Richard Jefferies claimed that thirty post-human years were all that was necessary for the tree line to march up the hills and reclaim the city. Brabsden Green is an experiment in such re-wilding. Within thirty years of Brabsden Green's dissipation, the casual passer-by would see no trace, though perhaps they would feel 'a sense sublime / of something far more deeply interfused.' Wordsworthian ruins, fifteen minutes' walk from the Central Line. Pace from the pre-Roman track at Brabsden Green to the Horsenden Hill crest and back, and you might see time as a loop — might catch a glimpse of London as the primeval weald not of its past, but of its future.

At the end of *Survival*, at the summit of Horsenden Hill, The

Doctor talks to Ace, who, through combat, has been infected with the essence of the Cheetah People.

"They've been taken back to the wilderness," he says, "the place is different, but the hunt goes on. You know all about the hunt, don't you Ace?"

"I felt like I could run forever," she says. "Like I could smell the wind and feel the grass under my feet and just run forever."

"The planet's gone," says The Doctor. "It lives on inside you. It always will."

Ace grins, stares, her eyes clouded over, just for a moment.
"Good."

NORTHALA FIELDS

Tim Cresswell

T he Eiffel Tower is 1,063 feet tall. Constructed in 1889 as part of the Paris World's Fair, for forty-one years it was the tallest manmade structure in the world. Discounting aerial masts and the occasional chimney it is still the second tallest in Europe. In the 1890s Edward Watkin decided to build his own tower to exceed the height of the Eiffel Tower. His structure, to be constructed in a pleasure park to the northwest of London in Wembley, would be 150 feet higher than the Eiffel Tower. He even asked Gustave Eiffel to design it. Eiffel refused on patriotic grounds.

Watkin was an MP and railway entrepreneur and chairman of the Metropolitan Railway that had made its way to the bucolic setting of Wembley. Wembley Park station had opened in 1893. He was a space maker – spreading London out horizontally and attempting to do the same vertically. The finished tower was due to feature astronomical observation desks benefiting from the clear air that exists at such lofty altitudes. Punters who wanted to gain the best views of London would have to take the Metropolitan Line out to Wembley Park before ascending a tower that would have been taller than The Shard.

Such altitudes were never reached. Watkin's tower became Watkin's Folly as only its initial, squat stage was ever finished – at a fairly unspectacular 154 feet. The existing structure, suffering from subsidence, was dynamited in 1907 as it had become a safety hazard. For the most part, it disappeared from Londoners' imaginative horizons.

Another climb that you cannot make in present day London is the climb to the top of the old Wembley Stadium's twin towers. These towers were a mere 35 metres high and entirely made of concrete. Between 1923 and 2003 they symbolized the *home of football*. Like the Eiffel Tower, Wembley Stadium was always supposed to be temporary — a part of the British Empire Exhibition of 1924/25. It was saved from demolition and became the national stadium and site of England's 1966 World Cup victory over Germany (as well as many defeats — including the last match — a more representative 1-0 loss to Germany). As it turns out, Wembley Stadium (Mark I) was temporary after all. The stadium was demolished in 2003 to make way for Wembley Stadium (Mark II).

In order to make the new stadium the pitch had to be lowered. During the excavation work necessary for this the workers had discovered the concrete footings to Watkin's Tower which has been on the exact site of the football pitch before the stadium was constructed. These had to be dug out in order to successfully construct the site for the new turf. Briefly, Watkin's Tower had an afterlife with national newspapers reflecting on the failed attempt to outdo the Eiffel Tower. *The Guardian* told the story of Watkin's Folly under the title 'The Height of Ambition' (13th March 2006). The failure of the tower became a metaphor for architectural hubris and the constant overruns that the new construction was suffering from. The new stadium was completed, several years late, in 2008. Its highest point is a triumphant 440 feet arch which is visible across west London. To the best of my knowledge, this is another climb you cannot make.

I have travelled the A40 into London countless times, starting with the time I came into London to catch the coach from Waterloo back out to my Inner London Education Authority run boarding school near Ipswich. Later it would be the route for trips to and from my student 'digs' in Finsbury Park and Crouch End. Most recently it has been the way to and from my parents' house in Carterton, Oxfordshire — best known for being close to RAF Brize Norton, which was where my dad worked for many years of his life.

One of the landmarks along the route is RAF Northolt, once the home of Hurricanes stationed there to defend London during the Battle of Britain and now the home to the Royal Air Force Queen's Flight. Being the son of an RAF engineer I always noticed RAF Northolt. I could tell you about the Andovers the Queen's Flight used and how they were replaced by BAE 146s and how these were later rebadged as AVRO regional jets — the last commercial airliner to be designed and built entirely by the British aircraft industry. I always had the *Observer's Book of Aircraft* for Christmas. Updated every year.

I am consistently amused by the short lampposts that line the A40 as you pass the end of the runway. They serve as one of my markers for entry into London. Passing the M25 is one of them — and the next are the dwarf lamp posts. These are followed by the Hoover Building. What you are unlikely to notice anywhere near the airbase are planes landing or taking off. I have never seen a plane land or take off despite years of driving past. Back in the 1960s a pilot, mistaking the runway for Heathrow, landed a 707 on its comparatively short airstrip. Over the years this story became one in which a much bigger 747 landed on it only to discover it was too heavy to take off again. That story is not true.

Northolt is described as a dormitory suburb of Ealing, itself a suburb of London (to Ealing residents it is THE suburb of London — the "Queen of Suburbs"). Northolt is a suburb of a suburb. If you look Northolt up on Google you will discover that it was the home of the bassist from Gary Numan's 'Tubeway Army'. So, the airport is pretty much the only thing Northolt is remarkable for, and even that is really not in Northolt but neighbouring Ruislip. As you move along the A40, or Western Avenue, as it is known by the time it reaches Northolt, you will catch glimpses of Wembley's already-iconic arch to the north.

Wembley's arch rose into view from the A40 in 2006. Since 2008 there has been another addition to the sights which mark entry into London. Not long after passing the aerodrome, on the opposite side to the stadium, you see four smooth, grass-covered mounds. It is not immediately clear what they are. They are at once bucolic and green yet clearly artificial in their symmetrical perfection. They resemble oversized tumuli — postmodern burial mounds; turfed-up, beautified slag heaps; or the giant salt hills that line American midwestern interstates waiting for the inevitable snow. They seem to refer, in a miniaturized-computer-game-simulation-Teletubbies-kind-of-way, to the Chilterns and Cotwolds out west, beyond the M25.

This is Northala Fields. The mounds and the surrounding park are a piece of land art created by the artist Peter Fink and the landscape architect Igor Marko. It is, in fact, Europe's largest example of land art. It is also a park — an urban amenity — that shields nearby houses from the drone of the A40.

Demolishing a grand building such as Wembley Stadium

brings with it a number of problems. Wembley is no longer a bucolic Middlesex village and there is no convenient old quarry where the rubble can be tipped and buried. 65,000 lorry loads of concrete had to go somewhere. Each lorry load cost money and each mile that each lorry travelled would add to the ballooning cost of the new structure that would rise on the same site. Some of that rubble was the remains of the footings from Watkin's Tower.

The neat solution to this problem was to move the rubble just a few miles south to Northolt. The tumuli of Northala Fields contain the concrete from the old Wembley Towers (and soil excavated during the construction of Westfield Mall in Shepherd's Bush) and thus something of the World Cup final of 1966 or Live-Aid concert of 1985. Just as our prehistoric ancestors gathered at Stonehenge with some sense of the sacred, perhaps we can enact pilgrimages to these postmodern, computer-designed, perfectly symmetrical mounds in respect for the stories carried by the concrete walls that line the corkscrew path which invites families to climb after Sunday dinner.

The medieval monk, translator of Aristotle and teacher of Thomas Aquinas, Albertus Magnus, wrote in his work *De Natura Locorum* (On the Nature of Places) that everything from people to stones have a natural place — a place where they belong. When things are dislocated and misplaced they lose their strength and identity he wrote — even stones become weak when moved beyond their proper place.

On the other hand there are always those who believe that objects have something of the *genius loci* or 'spirit of place' about them. When an object moves it carries this spirit with it. Perhaps rocks have stories. Why else would people gather in museums to look at, and touch, rocks brought back from the moon? Moon rocks look and feel pretty much like earth rocks. But we think something of the moon or, perhaps, the voyages to and from the moon, will rub off on us just by being in their vicinity. We know where they came from and that is enough. This is voodoo we can believe in — even when the rocks are concrete.

One of the most important moments in the making of place is its naming. Someone (or some sub-committee) chose not to call these mounds "Northolt Hills". The word "fields" is slightly curious here used, as it is, for what are clearly "hills". "Fields" suggests something flat and more expansive to me — unless we think of them as playing fields perhaps. The choice of the name "Northala" suggests a connection to a history that Northolt seems to be particularly devoid of. The name Northala turns up in the Domesday Book in reference to the area now known as Northolt. This used to be a manor bestowed by William the Conqueror on Geoffrey de Mandeville, Sherriff of Middlesex and Constable of the Tower. While Northholt means "North Wood", Northala means "North Hall". In this way Northolt is connected to Southall (which was called Southolde in 1610). A footnote in the *Home Counties Magazine: Devoted to the Topography of London, Middlesex, Essex, Herts, Bucks, Berks, Surrey and Kent*, Volume VIII from 1906 tells us that "Neither Northolt nor Southall stands on a slope, nor is there any vestige of a hill between these two places." Thanks to Northala Fields this is no longer true.

The four mounds are 22 metres, 18 metres, 18 metres and 12 metres respectively. 70 metres in total. Exactly the same as the combined height of the old Wembley Stadium's twin towers.

The mounds of Northala Fields beg to be climbed. They draw in families on even the greyest of weekends. The spiral path that performs a gentle helter skelter up the highest mound allows you to climb up (complete with pushchair if necessary) but it is also possible to take a more direct route up and down the smaller mounds. Here, desire lines have been cut by repeated use — straight up and down the mound.

Climbing to the top of the highest mound brings together two activities most often held apart — walking and looking. Looking, we are told, is an act of mastery. Looking from a high point, in particular, is associated with a distanced and abstracted kind of masculine spatial imagination. The point of view of planners and other megalomaniacs. Walking, on the other hand, is full of wholegrain, relatively rebellious, goodness, often associated with the multitude of ways in which urban dwellers insist on not behaving themselves. Walking is the Bohemian pastime of psychogeographers. Looking is of the head while walking is of the body. Northala Fields manages to combine looking and walking in a structure that simply begs us to climb and then to look. To take in the view as we feel a slight increase in our rate of breathing. Northala Fields is hardly the Eiffel Tower.

In the seven years I lived in Acton I visited Northala Fields once. I had driven past it so many times I felt the need to see it up close. I wanted to climb to the top. I climbed the tallest mound with my family — my wife and I followed the curve up to the summit while the children made their own ways, taking shortcuts, being more direct. The angle of slope is perfect for slightly daring adventures rolling down the hill. This is best done on the smaller mounds, which do not have a ready made spiral path disrupting the downhill passage. They are also perfect for sledding on those days when the schools are closed and the country comes to a muffled standstill.

Despite its relatively diminutive height, the view from the top was a good one. This being Northolt, there were not many other tall structures to obstruct the view. We could look east across the flat, leafy expanse of London's western suburbs to central London and its proliferation of towers. We could see The Shard being built, the Post Office Tower, the London Eye and all the other structures whose names have not become so well known. Nearby you can see the golden arches of McDonalds. And to the north, the towering arch of the new Wembley Stadium itself arcs over a low hill which hides the body of the stadium from view.

MOUNT PLEASANT

Tamar Yoseloff

B ack in the mid-nineties, when I was living off the Gray's Inn Road, I routinely made the walk north-east from my flat to Islington. My route took me through Mount Pleasant, a strange name for a place that was downright dreary — simply a cut-through, a desire path to more salubrious parts. It felt a bit like an island, marooned in the centre of the city, its Babel the bleak grey sorting office that dominated the summit. But I could sense an energy rising up through the pavement, passing through my feet; some remnant of Mount Pleasant's distant past had grabbed me, halted me in my tracks. Yeats felt this too, the pull of the city's ruins over which we walk. 'This melancholy London,' he wrote, 'I sometimes imagine that the souls of the lost are compelled to walk through its streets perpetually. One feels them passing like a whiff of air.'

Later I realised it was the river I could sense, the once-great Fleet, forced underground. I was living on its shores in Clerkenwell, a place that takes its name from the springs along the river's banks.

> It flows beneath my feet, its subterranean banks
> unseen. I glide blissfully through my day,
> all liquid, like a fish. I can't understand
> what gives this extra lift to my step, as if I'm floating,
> and the cars drifting through Clerkenwell Green
> are barges carrying sailors home from sea.[1]

---

[1] From 'Fleet' by Tamar Yoseloff, published in *Sweetheart*, Slow Dancer Press, 1998.

Mount Pleasant was a vantage point, its name suggesting a lovely riverside view. But dig deeper and you find 'Mount Pleasant' was the local joke for a vast and growing rubbish heap. We've held onto the name for over three centuries, ensuring the site remains an anti-beauty spot. Its 'official' name was Coldbath Fields, after the spring discovered in 1697 (the year of Hogarth's birth); next to the rubbish heap was a health spa, a reputable establishment (unlike the bagnios to the south) providing remedial cold springs to cure any number of ailments:

> Dissiness, Drowsiness, and heavyness of the head, Lethargies, Palsies, Convulsions, all Hectical creeping Fevers, heats and flushings, Inflammations and ebullitions of the blood and spirits, all vapours, and disorders of the spleen and womb, also stiffness of the limbs and Rheumatick pains, also shortness of breath, weakness of the joints, as Rickets, etc., sore eyes, redness of the face, and all impurities of the skin, also deafness, ruptures, dropsies and jaundice. It both prevents and cures colds, creates appetites, and helps digestion, and makes hardy the tenderest constitution.[2]

Maybe it was the proximity of the refuse tip that made Coldbath Fields' citizens ill.

> *But an undercurrent sinks me at Islington:*
> *I sense the bones of the old prison, the plague-dead*
> *dumped straight from their beds, butchers' scraps*
> *staining the water blood red.*[3]

---

[2] *Post Boy*, 28th March 1700, as quoted by William Pinks in *The History of Clerkenwell* (London, Charles Herbert, 1881).

[3] 'Fleet'.

The old prison I mention in my poem was also called Coldbath — not a cure to mend your ails, but an icy plunge into purgatory. It could accommodate eighteen hundred inmates, making it the largest British prison of its day. Coleridge and Southey thought it the residence of the Devil:

> As he went through Coldbath Fields he saw
> A Solitary cell;
> And the Devil was pleased, for it gave him a hint
> For improving his prisons in Hell.[4]

It was a brutal place, its cells overcrowded and in poor condition. It became infamous for its treadwheel, built to grind corn, and powered by up to three hundred and fifty men trudging up and down along its revolving beam. Facing them was the motto on the workroom wall: 'Behold how good and pleasant it is for brethren to dwell in unity.' Pleasant. Devalued in the same way as nice. A euphemism for positively evil.

When I arrive in Mount Pleasant, not a lot is going on. Taxis race up the hill on their way to somewhere else. The sky is grey, like the drab woollen uniforms of Coldbath's inmates. This place is always grey, even in sun; but today there is no hint of sun, just a light drizzle. I am standing on the corner of what was formerly Dorrington Street, the original terrace erected in 1720 (about half a dozen houses are still standing), and Warner Street, outside the Apple Tree pub. The pub has been occupied of late by avant-garde poets, who hold monthly readings in its upstairs room; fitting, as it was the local

---

[4] Robert Southey & Samuel Taylor Coleridge, 'The Devil's Thoughts', in *The Poetical Works of Coleridge, Shelley, and Keats* (Paris, A. & W. Galignani, 1829).

hostelry of Henry Carey, Mount Pleasant's most famous bard, who wrote:

> See yonder river's flowing tide,
> Which now so full appears:
> Those streams, that do so swiftly glide,
> Are nothing but my tears.[5]

The Apple Tree was once the first stop for newly released prisoners; fake handcuffs were used for bell pulls on the taps. I sit on one of the pub benches, with a view down Warner Street, below Rosebery Avenue underpass with its ornate Victorian iron bridge. This is the border of the area once known as Hockley-in-the-Hole; 'hockley' was Saxon for 'muddy field', as the Fleet routinely flooded the neighbourhood. In 1710 Jonathan Swift wrote that the river was full of 'sweepings from butchers' stalls, dung, guts and blood.' A century later it was described as a 'sluggish and plague-breeding sewer.' Hockley was one of the most notorious areas of London, characterised by the historian Richard Tames as 'a miry tumble-down thoroughfare . . . where low life rarely came any lower.'

Hockley's greatest attraction was bear-baiting, but there were many other diversions. Sometimes the brawlers were women, forced to hold half-crown coins to prevent them from scratching each other. Sometimes dogs and bears fought with fireworks strapped to their backs. The landlord of the Coach and Horses was mauled and eaten by one of his own bears in front of a greedy audience. If you walk down Warner Street, you descend into the hole itself, a bowl-like depression in the street, and outside the Coach and Horses, you

---

[5] 'The Aviary: Or, Magazine of British Melody' (London, 1745).

can stand over a grate in the middle of the road and hear the Fleet swishing below — as prophesied, reduced to sewer.

Before me is the great bulk of the sorting office, which fills the footprint of the prison. In fact, it is like a prison, stark and huge. And like the prison, the sorting office has the distinction of being the largest in Europe. Next to it, across from where I'm sitting, is the Royal Mail car park, equally vast, and surrounded by a brick wall, which in turn is surrounded by a twisted metal fence. The car park is sunk several feet below street level; giving an idea of the true level of the river. Another descent. The car park is one of the last remaining undeveloped WWII bomb sites in central London. Mount Pleasant should be on the tourist route.

In 2012, Royal Mail announced that it was planning to sell off as much as half of the sorting office, creating a building plot of twelve acres for residential developments, potentially earning the Post Office up to one billion pounds. The then-shadow postal affairs minister, Ian Murray MP, said at the time:

> Rather than hundreds of millions of pounds they get from the sale of Mount Pleasant going back into Royal Mail following any sale, it'll go straight into the coffers of a private-equity company, no doubt into a tax haven.[6]

The privatisation of Royal Mail enabled the proposed sale to move forward. There have been serious accusations that the British public did not receive value for money when the company was floated on the London Stock Exchange. A public petition against privatisation stated that Royal Mail was worth an estimated twenty billion pounds,

---

[6] *The Guardian*, 14th May 2012.

but valued at just over three billion:

> The government is giving away a public utility so that large corporations can turn a profit. The public has not been consulted about this, it was not in any party manifesto. The sell-off is a travesty that must be stopped.[7]

Following flotation, the government holds a majority share of nearly forty per cent.

I stand across the road and stare into the parking lot, where weeds and trash are clinging to the periphery walls. It occurs to me that one way of summing up Mount Pleasant is to think again of the rubbish heap — its history is about containment: the containing of public waste, of illness, of convicts, of letters, of explosives, of poverty. Now what's being contained is wealth, potentially billions, which might transform this provisional place into a destination, assigning it a new and prosperous future which will no doubt neatly cover up the past (like every hospital and factory that converts itself into luxury flats). The shift began with that first neat white modern luxury apartment block on Warner Street, and moves progressively, wiping Hockley and Coldbath into the sewers of the Fleet. But that's change, the way all cities cover and contain their past, something new and bright rising from the ashes of what's gone before.

> *The old dark brick*
> *shifts, the city groans in its foundations*
> *and spits me out like a sour grape into the street.[8]*

---

7   38 Degrees Campaign petition, November 2013.
8   'Fleet'.

WINDMILL HILL

Matt D. Brown

H ave you ever followed your shadow up a mound of shit and bone? Finsbury Square, late Autumn, 1pm. Low sunbeams head north along the ancient line of Moorgate and Finsbury Pavement. I'm blocking their way, and a long shadow, four times my height, commands the ground before me. It points uphill, ever so slightly. I suspect few people ever notice the gradient.

This is Tabernacle Street, a road typical of the City fringes. Victorian warehouses square up with 1960s derelicts and modern office blocks. Approaching from the south, one enters a shadowy canyon, its pavements cracked from the weight of a thousand heavy goods vehicles, squeezing through to infill sites, such as the hole where a restaurant-bar called The Prophet burned down in 2010. Fire is a frequent visitor to this hill, as we shall see.

At first, Tabernacle Street, at least its southern stretch, appears to be one of London's least interesting streets. It contains no shops, no homes, a solitary tree and just as many people. It is an entirely manmade environment, whose pavements receive only a couple of hours' sunlight each day. Even the slope of Tabernacle Street is artificial. If I'd walked this way five hundred years ago, I'd have been several metres lower and thigh-deep in water.

For much of its history, this was a sodden, flat place known as Moorfields, an extra-mural mulch with few tracks or buildings. Yet the land was not useless. The marsh served as a source of fish and fowl for medieval Londoners, and provided reeds to thatch their homes. It acted as an obstacle to stymie invading armies. In winter it would freeze, to the amusement of London's youth, who would slip and slide on primitive ice skates. It was also used as a dump. The marsh, in turn, was probably manmade. Construction of the city walls in Roman times is thought to have dammed a source stream of the River Walbrook, causing it to back-up and flood these Finsbury fields. As London grew, the marsh was drained and filled with gravel and other detritus. The drier ground became noted for archery practice. Target butts would stretch across the fields, into pastures beyond Old Street. If you look upwards while passing PC World on Chiswell Street, you'll spy a stone-carved archer, commemorating this pastime.

The moors were drained and filled, but in places they also began to rise. According to 16th century historian John Stow, the area I'm approaching, north of Finsbury Square, was 'so overheightened with lay-stalls of dung, that now three windmills are thereon set'. Stow also makes reference to 'Some thousands of [carriage] loads and more of human bones,' which were dumped in the same area following a clear-out of St Paul's charnel house around 1550.

This hill I'm climbing, then, is the ultimate manmade structure: an abominable accretion of dead Londoners, steeped in the shit of their descendants; a vast necrocopia, faecally fixed in a morbid mordant, and posing as a natural feature. I shall be careful where I tread.

The western parts of this ghastly mound were called Bone Hill, later corrupted to Bunhill. The eastern end, thanks to its landmark structures, became Windmill Hill. While Bunhill Fields is well known, you've perhaps not heard of Windmill Hill. Nobody's heard much of it since the 18th century, when it became Windmill Street and then, a century later, Tabernacle Street. But the slope is still there, and I'm climbing it now in search of its hidden history.

About half-way up, a nondescript office bears a fading black plaque: 'Forty yards south of this building on the east side was the site of The Foundry,' it informs me. I look around, and mentally pace the distance back down the hill to the junction with Bonhill Street (another corruption of Bone Hill). A derelict, cream building sports conflicting signs, suggesting that it is both 'to let' and 'under demolition'. It is, I think, one of the sorriest looking buildings in the whole of London. It can't even be trusted to hold its own plaque.

The Foundry, which stood here from 1684, was an important gun manufacturer, supplying cannons for the Crown. It was conveniently placed, just a two-minute walk from the barracks of the Honourable Artillery Company, still present on City Road next to Bunhill Fields. Tragedy struck in 1716 when the combination of molten metal and a damp mould led to a terrific explosion. According to a later newspaper account, 'It blew up with the greatest violence, tearing up the ground some feet deep, breaking down the furnace, untiling the house, and killing many people on the spot with the streams of melted metal.' For some weeks afterwards, the Bills of Mortality noted further casualties who died from head wounds from the hot metal. In total, seventeen people lost their lives, including a number of dignitaries and master of the foundry Matthew Bagley. This was one of the worst explosions in London's history up to that point. It prompted the removal of all artillery manufacturing to Woolwich. The incident is all but forgotten today.

Yet out of this carnage came something remarkable.

Twenty-three years later, a certain John Wesley took possession of the damaged factory and converted it into the London headquarters for his nascent Methodism movement, retaining its name as The Foundry (or The Foundery). Here Wesley would preach to crowds of several thousand. It is this association that the nearby plaque records, as well as the death of Wesley's mother in the same building. That one location should be the site of such a powerful disaster, and a foundation stone of a religion that now has eight million adherents is remarkable, especially when you see the apathetic building that stands on this site today.

The great explosion was just one of many fiery incidents on this hill of bone. In 1768, a Mrs Morgan, mother of a famous highwayman who had recently escaped from Newgate Gaol, fell into a fit, then fell into her fire. She perished. In 1833, five-year-old John Spellman was left home alone and set fire to his clothes, with fatal results. Eight years later and two more people were killed in a fire at the local swimming baths further along the street. Children aged eleven and twelve succumbed to fire within months of one another in 1865, and two women were severely burned at a tobacconist's the year after.

The area is charged with fire and sparks. Thousands camped out here in 1666 after escaping the Great Fire of London. The Christmas cracker was invented a few streets away by Tom Smith, but his factory burnt to the ground in 1889. The hill was pummelled in the Blitz, its craters and blasted buildings memorably captured on canvas by Cyril Mann. One bomb site remains as a car park on the northern slope of the hill. Even Wesley played with sparks. He was fascinated by the nascent science of electricity, and advocated electrification as an effective remedy for all manner of ailments. A curious note in the *Newcastle Courant* of 30th August 1760 reveals that a valuable horse was led to Wesley's Foundry to be electrified, "The effect of which, is not yet made publick".

After all this hot work, I need a drink. Towards the top of the hill, I discover The Windmill pub, a vestigial reminder of Tabernacle Street's past. We can see windmills on this hill in the earliest maps of London, drawn in the 1550s. A view from one hundred years later shows six windmills cramped together on the slopes, and some remained until the 18th century.

The Windmill pub is their last remnant, and has existed since at least 1865, when the body of thirty-four year-old William Braddock was found in a closet, his throat slit by his own hand. The pub's history is otherwise of little note, except to mention that the landlord in 1915 had the unfortunate name, for one who serves gassy drinks, of Ernest Belcher. To avoid a similar outcome, I enjoy my refreshing half pint at a leisurely pace, while studying the wall decorations. A generic watercolour of a windmill is partnered with a fascinating Victorian photograph of the pub, complete with horse-drawn vehicles and ornate lamps.

The fabric of the building has changed little in the intervening years, but the clientele are cut from a very different cloth. In the 19th century, The Windmill would have served its best to a local working class population of furniture makers, tailors and other craftsmen. It was a shabby area. An inquiry into road widening in 1867 noted that the housing was 'not even third class', and cases of bankruptcy, petty theft and the 'sale of watered down milk' are common. But the street was not without people of initiative. Newspaper adverts of 1864 boast of an 'improved sausage cutting and making machine' available from A. Lyons at number thirty-two. Today, the area is given over to small start-up firms, and medium-sized enterprises cocooned in offices. I work in one myself, a few street to the north-east.

I leave the pub and crest the hill. It now slopes down towards Old Street. This stretch passes behind Wesley's Chapel, the sequel to The Foundry, which offered the preacher more space when he moved his church here in 1778. It is a strange sight, peering into its back yard from Tabernacle Street. A scattering of grave stones nestle beside stowed electrical equipment and bin bags. The 18th century dead must share their ground with trappings of the 21st century. The vault of Wesley himself can be seen, surmounted by a monument that looks not unlike the eccentric spire of nearby St Luke's church. I'm not stopping today, but the attached building contains a museum to Methodism and what must be London's most ornate gents toilet.

I continue down the north slope of the hill. On my right are further contradictory signs: "Friendly House" paired with "You are being watched on CCTV". I pass the former Paradise Street, another religious remnant. Next comes the McQueen bar, named after the famous actor whose likeness is plastered throughout its dining room. This is the only building on the entire street that might be described as stylish. It opened a few years back, replacing an older pub with the much more site-specific name of The Tabernacle.

The final building of note is a great stone pile in Victorian Gothic, now part of the Central Foundation Boys' School. This was the site of yet another religious gathering place, this time centred on Wesley's friend George Whitefield. Whitefield's Tabernacle was the building that gave this street its name, and lasted until 1907 when the Methodist congregation moved to Alexandra Palace.

Having reached its bottom, I leave the hill and pass on to flatter ground to the north, a plain that once whistled with arrows. I contemplate the singular history of the mound behind me. Men came and blocked a river creating a marsh. Into that marsh they heaped bodies and excrement, until the land rose into an artificial mound. On that mound stood windmills and tabernacles. The land was scoured with fires and explosions, but blessed with the Word of God and the rise of a new religious movement. And now it is largely forgotten, to the point where the hill itself is rarely noticed.

From plain to swamp to hill to nought, what awaits this protean land of windmills, fire and sermon? You have only to wander a few streets away to imagine. All around Tabernacle Street, modern blocks of glass, steel and stone are forming. Our hill sits within a deep invagination of the Square Mile's boundaries. Head east or west and you'll find yourself under the jurisdiction of the City of London. As the City pushes ever-outwards, replacing tired warehouses with smart office blocks, how long before the pocket closes and these streets are subsumed in a final stage of phagocytosis?

There are no listed buildings or preservation orders on Tabernacle Street. It will be a very different place in twenty-five years. But those future tenants and office workers will always be anchored in shit, bone and ash.

SNOW HILL

Tom Chivers

A s the train pulls away from the new platforms of Farringdon, I bring my face close to the window of the carriage, cup my hands and squint into the hurtling dark. I know what I am looking for, but not whether I will find it.

A young woman with a bulldog snuffling between her feet throws me a suspect glance. And then, in an instant, the tunnel wall recedes and for no more than a second or two the empty concrete platform of an abandoned station appears before me, cast in the pale glow of security lights. I barely have time to register the thrill before the tunnel narrows again and the train races on through City Thameslink and Blackfriars, where I alight to the silver landscape of the river. I had set out to climb a hill, but I was already sidetracked. London does that. It's a city of digressions.

What I had glimpsed in the darkness of that tunnel were the remains of Snow Hill Station, later known as Holborn Viaduct Low Level. Now forgotten by all but the dedicated *gricer*, Snow Hill opened in 1874 on the City line between Ludgate Hill (now City Thameslink) and Farringdon Street (now Farringdon). The Snow Hill Tunnel was a significant piece of London's railway infrastructure, connecting the overground into the City with the Tube at Farringdon, with an additional branch carrying freight trains to yards underneath Smithfield Market. But the Station itself was underused and on 1st June 1916, as the Battle of Jutland raged in the North Sea, Snow

Hill Station closed its doors. The tunnel survived until the 1970s when it too lay derelict, its tracks ripped out like so much worthless guttering.

But the story didn't end there. When Snow Hill Tunnel re-opened in 1990 to service the new Thameslink line, the ghost platforms of its abandoned station remained: a subterranean glitch in a labyrinth of glitches, dead-ends, bricked-up portals. The city beneath.

I had come to climb a hill, to feel the city's natural topography, but I was just chasing a name. I returned on foot from Blackfriars, tracing the sewerised river Fleet upstream along Farringdon Road, all the way to the Holborn Viaduct. The last time I made this journey was the morning of the second day of my stag weekend, and I was violently sick underneath the arches of the Viaduct. This time, sober enough, I stop to photograph boarded-up doorways, and wrought iron gates guarding dead spaces full of leaves and junk. (One conceals a mysterious service staircase and a discarded cardboard placard reading ARMY MOTHERS GRIEVE AS ONE / R.I.P. LEE RIGBY).

The land either side of Farringdon Road rises away from the valley of the Fleet in a chain of clay bluffs and gravel hills whose names have been retained in the streetplan. On the west side we have Saffron Hill, Herbal Hill, Back Hill, Vine Hill, Eyre Street Hill and Mount Pleasant, along with the obsolete Windmill and Holborn Hills. On the east side: Ludgate Hill, Snow Hill, and the sloping courses of Cowcross and Turnmill Streets (the former recalling the point at which cattle crossed the Fleet, the latter a watermill).

The Holborn Viaduct has spanned the Farringdon Road /

Fleet valley since 1869, and recently received a gleaming new paint job. With the Victorian's enthusiasm for monolithic engineering solutions, the Viaduct blast a ruler-straight track through the natural terrain of the city; connecting the summits of Snow and Holborn Hills and making right the alignment of the road with Watling Street / via Trinobantina. (You can still drive all the way from here to Chiswick Common in a straight, Roman line.)

To stand on the Viaduct and look down over Farringdon Road is to experience London's vertical axis; the city not as streetplan writ large, but a three dimensional environment with depth as well as spread. And even to the untrained eye, the view from the Viaduct is unmistakeably that of a river from a bridge. The traffic rumbles past, oblivious to the rush and gurgle of the Fleet twenty or thirty feet below.

Every Sunday at 10.55 a.m. I cross the Holborn Viaduct on my way to Mass at St Etheldreda's, the former chapel of the Bishop of Ely in London. As I power-walk from Newgate, Snow Hill is just that enigmatic side-street falling away from the level. I have never tried to connect it up. But today is different. I have come to make an ascent.

The foot of the hill is a few yards north of the Viaduct's stone pillars on Farringdon Road, where West Smithfield climbs at a right angle from the valley, with the boarded-up facade of the disused General Market arranged along it. (This historic structure is currently under threat of demolition by the Corporation of London; a story to be told another time.) The road that calls itself Snow Hill forks south-east, twisting back towards Newgate, its route lined with parked cars. From certain angles, the hill appears to extend beneath street level, plunging down a steep vehicle ramp into the belly of the abandoned Market. A mountain born of the darkness, emerging from the ground. A couple of railwaymen in bright orange workwear and hard hats saunter past, talking rapidly in Spanish. They descend the ramp, and I spot a sign emblazoned with Crossrail logos and indicating the entrance to 'Snow Hill Basement'. The Basement was once the Smithfield railway sidings, later a vast underground car park, and has now been commandeered by the engineers and heavy lifters of Europe's largest infrastructure project: another tunnel for the tangled Farringdon intersection. Two more workers sit in a makeshift sentry box and their indifferent nods confirm the Crossrail story. I turn away and start my ascent.

Like so many of these flattened, tarmac-smoothed Fleet valley bluffs, Snow Hill is no more than a gentle incline; my calves barely register the effort to walk it. William Blake described it as 'almost level and … a very handsome street'.[1] But for Dickens, that exemplary urban cartographer, its slopes could still be precipitous to the careless driver.

> Near to the jail, and by consequence near to Smithfield, and on that particular part of Snow Hill where omnibuses going eastward seriously think of falling down no purpose, and where horses in hackney cabriolets going westward not unfrequently fall by accident, is the coachyard of the Saracen's Head Inn.[2]

Right on cue, a silver Mercedes turns in from Smithfield Street and

---

[1] Letter from William Blake to William Hayley, 26th October 1803.
[2] Charles Dickens, *The Life and Adventures of Nicholas Nickleby* (London, 1838).

accelerates towards me. It's not hard to imagine schoolchildren tobogganing down Snow Hill, but in fact its name is a corruption: it has nothing to do with snow. In 1598 John Stow identified it as 'Snore Hill', whilst it appeared as 'Snowr Hill' in 1504. The name appears to derive from the Old English toponym *snōr* meaning 'a bend in a road ascending a hill'.[3] For that is exactly what Snow Hill is, and the crook or bend in the road would have been more pronounced in the past than it is today. As old maps of London illustrate, the present alignment is much altered since the hill was the principal route down to the Fleet crossing at Holborn (or 'Oldbourne') Bridge. Snow Hill offered what one town planner described as a 'sinuous continuation'; the 'organic informality' of its twisting course in stark contrast to the Victorian monumentalism of the Viaduct.[4]

Even if that great age of urban terraforming is over, the city remains a place of constant change. The south side of Snow Hill is currently dominated by tall white hoardings surrounding a derelict plot: a temporary pocket of air in a dense urban environment. Opposite the hoardings, what was once another fine, red-brick edifice is enclosed in scaffolding and wears a kind of green veil — presumably to protect pedestrians from falling masonry.

I'm taking it slowly. Very slowly. As if by decreasing my rate of climb I might compensate for the brevity of the ascent. If you were to observe from any one of the several security cameras covering the

---

[3] Keith Briggs, ' Old English *snyring*, *snēring* 'steep place', *Notes and Queries* (September, 2010). Briggs attributes this etymology to Margaret Gelling.
[4] Corporation of London (Department of Planning), *Newgate Conservation Area Character Study* (1999).

road, you might even say I was dawdling. I have known mountains — real mountains. Felt the constriction of breath, the light-headedness of high altitude. Coughed up blood at five thousand metres. But this — so negligible a hillock I almost feel sorry for it. I want to climb the road like a mountain, squeeze a cam into a fissure in the pavement, tether my rope to a lamppost, bivouac by the bike rack.

The story of a mountain is the story of the people who have climbed it — the visionaries, dreamers and fools. I remember, traversing the snowy wastes of Thorong La, Nepal in my late teens, passing the makeshift grave of Rick Allen, overcome by Acute Mountain Sickness on 21st February 1991. Snow Hill, too, has its ghosts. The celebrated portrait-painters van Dyck and William Dobson, meeting in the latter's attic lodgings. John Bunyan succumbing to fever at the sign of the Star, August 1688. Thomas Johnson — botanist, Royalist soldier — busy in his apothecary's shop. And Austin Osman Spare, artist and student of the occult, entering the world in a rotten tenement by the King's Arms.

About half way up the Hill, a narrow path forks off to the left — Cock Lane. Somewhere at this junction once stood the Holborn Conduit: originally constructed in 1498 and rebuilt by William Lamb in 1577, after which it was called Lamb's Conduit. (The water flowed to Snow Hill in a lead pipe from present-day Lamb's Conduit Street.) An engraving of 1810 shows a handsome stone structure decorated with columns and an insignia of the City of London. The structure is topped with a miniature lamb and at its base fresh water gushes from the mouth of a lion. It is easy to forget that this part of London was once peppered with natural springs; the Fleet itself was known as 'the river of wells'.

Here, too, commuters once filed out of Snow Hill Station.

One photograph from 1901 shows the entrance — a dark, foreboding void — and above it a sign for 'South Eastern & Chatham & Dover Railways'. A figure is grappling with a newspaper which entirely covers his face and torso. It looks like the entrance to a ghost train ride, with this figure as its sinister operator.

The late afternoon sunlight catches on the tower of St Sepulchre-without-Newgate; its distinctive crown of four spires appears, from down here, to be ablaze. The siting of St Sepulchre — known as 'the musicians' church' — at the crest of Snow Hill has the visual effect of extending the Hill beyond its summit. The natural and the manmade conspire to enhance the city's vertical axis, just as they do in the case of Ludgate Hill and St Paul's Cathedral.

There has been a church on this site since Saxon times, when it was dedicated to St Edmund — the ninth century king of East Anglia who was reputedly decapitated by Viking leader Ivar the Boneless for refusing to renounce Christ. During the Crusades of the twelfth century, the church was renamed St Edmund and the Holy Sepulchre after the Church of the Holy Sepulchre in Jerusalem. And so a little piece of the Holy City could be transposed onto a patch of ground just outside the walls of London. (The Norman crypt of the nearby Priory Church of the Order of St John goes one step further — its altar contains a single stone physically removed from the Holy Sepulchre.) If you believe the myth, then the Church of the Holy Sepulchre marks the precise location of the Crucifixion — a rocky outcrop known as Calvary or Golgotha, *the place of the skull*. In the association of its summit with the Holy Sepulchre, Snow Hill offers a faint echo of Golgotha, rendering my ascent a kind of accidental pilgrimage.

I stop to photograph the handsome Victorian shopfront of

John J. Rosie of Manchester — inventor of the self-pouring teapot — before continuing my climb past Snow Hill Police Station (built in the 1920s on the site of the Saracen's Head inn). Tea, beer, spring water — everything flows here, on a hill shaped by a river. In his poem 'A Description of a City Shower' (1710) Jonathan Swift casts London not as New Jerusalem but as locus for the Flood, with Snow Hill at its centre. A vengeful God drowning the city in its own gory debris.

> Now in contiguous Drops the Flood comes down,
> Threat'ning with Deluge this devoted Town.
> ...
> Now from all Parts the swelling Kennels flow,
> And bear their Trophies with them as they go:
> Filth of all Hues and Odours seem to tell
> What Street they sail'd from, by their Sight and Smell.
> They, as each Torrent drives, with rapid Force,
> From Smithfield or St. Pulchre's shape their Course,
> And in huge Confluent join'd at Snow-Hill Ridge,
> Fall from the Conduit, prone to Holbourn-Bridge.
> Sweeping from Butchers Stalls, Dung, Guts, and Blood,
> Drown'd Puppies, stinking Sprats, all drench'd in Mud,
> Dead Cats and Turnip-Tops come tumbling down the Flood.

The Church of the Holy Sepulchre is also believed to be the burial place of Christ. At the centre of the great *rotunda* pilgrims wait in line to enter, crouched, a tiny chamber known as the Tomb of Jesus. Later they climb to another chapel run by Greek Orthodox; they kneel and kiss a silver disc marking the exact spot of the Crucifixion. The natural rock face of Golgotha is viewed through a glass screen, and pilgrims can touch the rock through an opening. One floor below, the rock can again be viewed, this time in the Chapel of Adam, supposedly the burial place of the first human. A rupture in the rock is said to have been caused by an earthquake during the Crucifixion.

> Jesus, when he had cried again... and the earth did quake, and the rocks rent. (Matthew 27:51)

As I reach the summit of Snow Hill, where a lone bus makes its way east across the Viaduct towards the West End, I wonder what dark mysteries are hidden within this urban mountain. Deep in its interior: the mechanised diggers of Crossrail mulch the earth; and an abandoned station, half-lit, is glanced from a speeding train.

LUDGATE HILL

Alan Cunningham

The Irish word for mountain is *sliabh*. At some point in time it — like so many other Irish words — was Anglicised to the Hiberno-English hybrid *slieve*. I have no issue with this process of transformation. Although I was taught the Irish language, briefly, at secondary school, I do not speak it.

In the area of Ireland where I was born and grew up, the word is much in use and there are many such 'slieves', a word I seldom hear or read in other places where English is spoken. There is Slieve Foy, for example, overlooking the narrow streets of Carlingford (the word is usually capitalised when used in conjunction with an actual peak, by the way, although this rule has some exceptions; in addition, and confusingly, sometimes the word is not used in relation to mountains at all); Slieve Donard, a little further away near Newcastle, the highest mountain in the Mournes range and the province of Ulster; and, much closer to home, Slieve Gullion, where I now recall that I spent many weekend mornings in my late teens, undertaking research for an obscure A-Level Geography project that I had convinced myself was about conservation. I can't remember now what it was really about, but I will always remember — or never forget, a different thing entirely — my time upon that mountain.

There are many other large hills and unusual geological features in the area — the Ring of Gullion stands out amongst them — all of which, combined with the larger mountains, give the area what I believe to be a slightly otherworldly feel. This, I accept, may be the result of having lived only in large cities since leaving Ireland. None of the peaks match the magnificence of anything in the Alps or Himalayas, of course, but they have a peculiar charm and precise beauty of their own. I imagine this effect to be especially strong in the mind of the local or locally born, confronted with them as they are — or having been confronted with them — on such a regular and unavoidable basis.

Many of these smaller peaks and hills were once topped off with temporary installations constructed by various regiments of the British Army. One such peak stands out in my memory: Crosslieve, or 'cross mountain', where one of the largest of the military camps in the area was based. There is no cross on this mountain. It is not even a mountain, it is a large hill. The base was dismantled some years back, I forget the precise details of when that happened and am not interested in looking up the date now. I don't even know if there was ever a cross upon that hill or how it got its name. I find it to be a strange presence in the area now. Prominent, somewhat beautiful: tainted land, to one who has the knowledge of what was once upon it. I have never been drawn to walk it. But, then, there are many such tainted features in the geography of where I grew up — if one chooses to see them, of course — for the closest town to my parents' house is Newry and the area where they live is on the eastern edge of South Armagh.

My father, Malachy, like his own father before him, was an electrician; he is retired now. My grandfather worked for most of his life at Horrockses, a cotton-spinning plant in Newry. It ceased operating under that name in the early 60s and became instead Ulster Textiles. My father worked abroad, mostly, although I am sure there are periods when he worked in Ireland, before I was born and when I was very young.

The justification behind the continual emigration of the Irish worker has always been the fact of a lack of work in Ireland. A sluggish economy. This was especially so in the Ireland of the 1970s and 80s; perhaps even for part of the early 90s. The boom that followed has been well documented, although the present economic climate in Ireland is as inclement as that of the 80s. People who had returned are leaving again, along with a younger generation who never felt they would have the need to leave at all.

An economic basis for the flight of a people makes good sense, I suppose, and that is how I have always justified it. Perhaps, though, thinking about it now, people simply enjoy travelling or get sick of the place they come from, irrespective of economics. I don't know if my father would agree.

The places where he worked included Nigeria, Canada, Saudi Arabia and the Shetland Islands. The place where he spent most time abroad, however, was that particular part of the world where money can always be made and which was to become part of my own experience and history: The City — yes, the City — of London.

The first summer I went to London to work with my father I was eighteen, I think. I remember the night before I left: drinking in Belfast with a school friend of mine from South Armagh and a nurse, the elder sister of his absent girlfriend. They tried to convince me to get very drunk with them and go out. I had an early flight and knew, not really wanting to go to London, if I had a hangover, I might not go at all. I wanted to spend that summer with such friends, drinking, travelling. I did not want to go to London and work with my father.

I did not have much money, however, and in London I knew — I had been told, repeatedly — I would most certainly make plenty of that. I had a few more drinks and then I went to bed.

That first summer together we worked at the Broadgate Estate, in a part of the building used by a Swiss bank, UBS. I was only there for a couple of months and cannot remember much of the experience.

The next time, perhaps it was a year later, I went for longer. The city had frightened me that first time out. I was more used to the sight of green fields, mountains and few people, even in Belfast, where such things wait at the end of long avenues and streets to remind you of the smallness of the city and the relative immensity of raw land that lies around it. But I do remember that it had also intrigued me. I was curious to explore it further. My father was then working at the headquarters of Goldman Sachs. It was located, as it is now, on Fleet Street, in the former headquarters of *The Daily Telegraph* — the newspaper trade having long since left the shade of St Bride's for Wapping.

We would often walk to work, my father and I, our route sometimes quicker than the time it took the bus to get to the top of Fleet Street. We lived above a pub on Bermondsey Street called The Marigold, now The Hand & Marigold and a gastropub. It was not one then. Our walking route led us toward, along and across the great river: along Tower Bridge Road, left at Tooley Street to follow Tooley Street along under London Bridge — or was it up Duke Street Hill and over, I can't remember? — but on, anyway, to Montague Close, past Southwark Cathedral, past The Golden Hinde, past The Clink, to Clink Street and then all along Bankside. Under Southwark Bridge, past the construction of the Tate Modern, past the construction of the Millennium Bridge, all the way to Blackfriars Bridge and up, and over the bridge, and up New Bridge Street and left and then: Fleet Street.

Work involved hosting the store in the basement, giving out materials to electricians, labourers, chippies, banksmen. Or, occasionally, riding up in the service elevator to assist an electrician in a job that required a mate. I wasn't much of a mate, but my father was right: I did like having the money and the job.

One Friday our boss called some of us into his office. He was a grey haired and unhealthily skinny arthritic who smoked Rothmans incessantly and drank pint after pint of creamy Guinness in the bar after work. He had once been a member, so the rumour went, of the SAS. He informed us of a change in our working habits. The week after, he told us, we would have to walk down Fleet Street, up Ludgate Hill and past St Paul's to a building on a street called Carter Lane, where Goldman Sachs had another trading office.

'There's a job needs doing', he said, puffing away.

And so we did as he had told us to, that next Monday, after clocking in. That first walk up we followed the directions we had been given. Down the remainder of Fleet Street, across Ludgate Circus, up the steep incline of Ludgate Hill and on towards St Paul's. Past the immensity of the Cathedral and along St Paul's churchyard, then right towards Carter Lane, the top end, up by the space of the Gardens.

Ludgate Hill. I remember as I walked up it I thought, *What colour is the soil beneath this road? What has grown here?* It was the relative effort of the climb, I suppose, that made me think such things. At that point, my legs had seldom been taxed by the elevation of a street in London. My walking experiences had been confined, for the most part, to flat streets and bridges. There had been stairs and steps, of course, but one expects a degree of strain in climbing such things. To find, on walking on a busy city street, that one is slowly moving upwards, rising above other streets; to find that one is looking back at them and that all sense of perspective is now skewed: it is an experience that prompts reflection on one's surroundings. It is an experience that prompts reflection on where, exactly, one is.

There is a story that Ludgate is so called because it was built by King Lud. I have little faith in such myths. Pevsner has it that the name of the hill comes from the Old English *hlid-geat*, from *hlid* (opening) and *geat* (passage). This word can be translated into contemporary English as meaning either swing gate or postern. I prefer to interpret it as postern. A back door. A private door.

Postern: from *posterus*, that which is subsequent.

From *post*, that which is after.

That evening, as I left the building we had worked in, I thought about taking the same route back to Fleet Street. I saw, however, and took, a different route. I saw that Carter Lane had much more presence in the City than we had experienced during our ascent. I saw a street leading somewhere unknown. There is something about catching sight of a path or a lane in a city — an unknown lane or path, you understand — that provokes in me the desire for exploration. I had learned that much during my time in London. So I walked along the rest of Carter Lane. It ran down behind the mess of buildings that sat opposite St Paul's and came out, via the tributary of Pilgrim Street, on to New Bridge Street. More interesting, however, were the streets that ran off of it.

Creed Lane.
Friar Street.
Addle Hill.
Ireland Yard.
Wardrobe Place.

I was fascinated by this tight collection of paths. They were not streets, no. Not in the London sense. Wandering them provided me with a feeling of calm in the busy city, for they were very quiet. But a quiet street in a busy city is a beautiful thing. The great gold cross that topped St Paul's loomed over them all, a reference point to take me back toward the City. Perhaps this is an embellishment, I admit. Perhaps that cross could not be seen in those streets at all, if I remember correctly.

Years later, I returned to those narrow streets around St Paul's Cathedral — and to St Paul's itself — carrying a video camera that I had recently bought and was then experimenting with. I was captivated again by the gold cross mounted on the top of the Cathedral and, on that day, the particular blue of the sky behind it. The narrow streets, the colour of the sky, the gold cross: all of it offered, I believe I thought that day, something of the same beauty I now recall when I think about those mornings on the summit of Slieve Gullion.

In my memory I am always walking towards a dark, copper coloured lake and a burial chamber that lie upon the peak. I am walking, but anxiously. I know I will soon have to descend to wait for my mother or my father — if he had been in Ireland — to drive me back home.

I have been walking those Irish mountains while writing this. I had to consult Pevsner to remind myself of the names of those London streets.

It has been so quiet here in Ireland. I rarely see anybody on my walks. There are no people in Ireland any longer, I feel, or, if there are, they have ceased walking. I had forgotten that fact but I remember it now. Those mornings on Slieve Gullion were always absent one thing: the presence of other people.

Being December and Ireland, it has often been grey, damp and cold. Last week was unseasonably warm, however, and I walked out one day on my route with more eagerness than usual. My route: up the back roads, towards the Bernish, from there past the Court Cairn, around by Seavers Road.

There is a forest to the right of the Bernish viewpoint. I have explored it many times. I have often reached the edge and looked out at the field that lies behind it. I have always thought: *that field must be the beginning of a route leading up to Camlough Mountain*. Last week, unaware of what I was doing, I walked through the small forest and made my way to the fence. I jumped over it, my curiosity growing. The weather, as I say, had been fine and the field was dry. I walked on, unsure of where I was going, but going ever upwards.

I soon arrived at a flat piece of land: a rest stop from the climb. It had once been artificially levelled, I realised, looking around, comparing. In contrast to its surroundings there was very little growing on it. Then I saw a path, also absent growth. I followed it, sure that it would lead me to the peak.

As I walked along, thankful for the path, I then thought perhaps it was a leftover from the removal of a military base. I had forgotten there had also been one on Camlough Mountain. *That piece of level land,* I thought: *that had been the site of a Sangar.* I looked down at the path. Maybe it was the result of the removal of the base. Maybe it had been the first stage in the construction of the same, now long gone and often forgotten.

NOTTING HILL

Inua Ellams

I stop when the colour and texture of the pavement changes and over my shoulder, directly behind, is High Street Kensington Tube station. Looking back, it must have seemed like a gateway to the Circle Line that runs through it (its bright yellow I must have associated with sunrise). Going through the barriers, the off-white stone slabs on the ground conjured up Dorothy's yellow brick road; and to look up as you make for the exit, the translucent dome of the roof, small, cathedral-like and holy, a slice of what I imagine the gateway to heaven looks like. These have stayed the same, everything else has changed: the shops inside the station are all different, the flow of energy, the speed of commuters spewing onto the streets is faster and I am different person. At the exit, a right turn falls away to Knightsbridge and Buckingham Palace. A left, and you face South Kensington and Hammersmith, but we always walked forward, always crossed the street. It was our only choice.

In 1996, when I arrived in London from Lagos, Holland Park School was the most multicultural in the area. It was so mixed that Nelson Mandela chose to visit a week or so before I joined. Perhaps Nelson saw the rainbow nation he wished for his country; perhaps he saw equality: us, rubbing shoulders in the quest for education and knowledge, lifting our collective consciousness merely by being around each other. But in the minutiae of school life, in the day-to-day of it all, it seemed we were anything but united. I wonder if a class divide existed then? It must have; something barely perceptible but definitely there, a cloud of concepts, notions and prejudices handed down from our parents, floating over the wide-eyed tribe of school kids exiting the station those mornings of discovery, mistakes and learning, negotiating ourselves past each other.

The cool kids ruled Notting Hill Gate and used that station, pouring in from Shepherds Bush, Ladbroke Grove and Queens Park. Once in a while, I'd come by bus. The closest stop was Sheffield Terrace and I'd disembark from the 52 and march up Bedford Gardens. Others would ride the 28, 27, 31, 49, 148 or 452 to peripheral stops dotted around the school. The wealthy ones who lived within walking distance would come by foot. I imagine we looked like a swarm of ants ascending up the hill in loose clusters, in stretched spirals, the brave young romantics in couples, all attempting to bury our insecurities, thinking of the day's events.

Those of us who had travelled by Tube, exiting at High Street Kensington, had three possible routes:

One. Cross the road, turn left down the High Street, get to Holland Park itself and walk through. Those who preferred a touch of greenery in the morning, a quick football match should four or more be gathered, would come this way and continue up, turning right at Campden Hill Street.

Two. Cross the road, turn right up Kensington Church Street past St Mary Abbots church and the monument to soldiers who died in the Great War. Those who liked the relative safety of main streets would come this way and continue the ascent by turning right at Sheffield Terrace.

Three. Cross the road onto Hornton Street, left at Holland, right to Camden Hill Road and a final left into Airlie Gardens. Those who wished for the mildly more adventurous would come this labyrinthine way to school. This was my journey.

At the corner of Hornton Street stood the magnolia tree. I'd always pause to kick it, thinking as the petals fell that they were lotus flowers and due to their oriental mystique I'd inherit something of Bruce Lee's powers. I'd walk on planning various ways to dispose of my enemies; who I'd karate-kick into the next week, who I'd one-inch-punch first and why. Meditating, I'd pass the majestic Kensington Central Library on the left, built in 1880. It was shelter from the rain and nothing else. Linked by its red bricks and the same sense of irrelevant majesty was the nearby Kensington Town Hall. Where the Library possessed something we'd occasionally, reluctantly agree could be beneficial to our continued harmony in school, the Town Hall was entirely impenetrable to us . It was where the adults went to be aggressively boring to one another. Years later, John — who played striker in class football games — and I would return to spend an afternoon aiming a ball at the No Ball Games sign drilled into the wall, waiting to be chased away, only to return and do it again.

After the Town Hall, I'd turn left onto Holland Street. Months later, this junction would become an occasional meeting place. Mo or Abdul, classmates who lived in South Kensington and Hammersmith, who'd come from the other end of the High Street but wished to avoid Holland Park, would wait. Our greetings were of the typical *hey, all right mate* variety. Now and then, we'd attempt a self-conscious high-five and miss each other's palms on purpose, laugh, then continue up hill, trading soft insults, recapping the previous day, what we'd watched on television, who fought whom and why. But in those first weeks at school, it was just me and the road, head down, shouldering past the Grade II listed block of flats, Academy Gardens. I'd imagine the wealthy inhabitants, who in my mind's eye were always pressed against the window, could see right through me, could tell that I didn't feel I belonged here. Months before a ball had rolled my way, which I'd kicked back with enough strength and precision to make John think me worth hanging with. He introduced me to the school's pecking order that first week. I grasped that my position was firmly at the bottom, that my thick Nigerian accent rendered me so. Regardless of what I said or how eloquent I said it, the accent was enough to send John and his various sidekicks into peals of rapid-fire laughter, finger-pointing, jeering, requests that I try to say it again, laughter anew, the sheer cyclicality of it all. These new classmates were Iranian, Algerian, Irish, English, Arabic, Scottish, Chinese, Pakistani, Indian, Bangladeshi, Jamaican, French, Moroccan, Spanish, Ghanaian and more. In Nigeria, all my classmates had been Nigerian. I would ascend, turn right onto Campden Hill Road, the penultimate street before school.

The final street was Campden Hill. I'd climb over the long wall that ran on its right side, drop down to the south playground of the school, where the gym and the swimming pool were situated, and take the connecting bridge over to the main grounds where the serious business of teaching was conducted. To walk down Campden Hill, I'd pass by property belonging to the Nigerian High Commission, a small fort of tall, black gates, a Nigerian flag flying at full mast, diplomatic car out front. Of the few lies I told in those first weeks — those attempts to seem larger (and cooler) than life — the biggest was a claim that the High Commissioner himself was a personal friend and if threatened I could go there, and because it was technically Nigerian soil, if any harm came to me on the premises, it would be deemed an Act of War. Of course, it never worked. I learnt the futility of diplomatic leverage when an apprentice bully kicked me to see what would happen. Like every other kid, I'd learn to fit in: I'd learn basic Cockney and the West London way of speaking English. I'd learn a new way of being.

School would finish at about three. For those enrolled in as many after-school extra-curricular activities as possible, school finished at four thirty or five, but we'd go home the way we'd come, descend the hill to our various stations and bus-stops, trading softer insults before the farewells. I'd reach High Street Kensington Station, dive underground and surface again at Victoria, a short walk from where I lived.

Once, though, after a good day when my shoulders broadened at a sudden compliment and a new friendship was successfully broached, I went to Notting Hill Gate instead. The friend lived somewhere that way. We left school, turned onto Campden Hill Road, right down Kensington Place past the rows of houses, pristine and perfectly arranged like iced loaves of bread — lotus flower trees in front. Somewhere by the primary school, I lost myself in the conversation. I forgot I wasn't in Nigeria anymore. We turned onto Hillgate Street and I lifted up a long thin branch from the roadside where it lay and swung it above my head, swung as we turned right at the Coronet Cinema, onto Notting Hill Gate. Metres from the station where I planned to leave the stick, we heard a siren. A police siren. A squad car pulled up, two officers got out and ran towards me. I stood terrified, rooted to the spot. They towered over me, demanding identification, asking what I intended to do with the weapon, where I had just come from, where I was going, for my name and address, yelling as they questioned. It never occurred to me to lie, to simply refuse to give my details, to argue or explain I'd done nothing wrong, that it wasn't an offence to hold a stick. Instead, I burst into tears on the road, begged for forgiveness, pleading with every fibre of my twelve-year-old body not to write my name in their black notebooks. I believed it meant I would have a criminal record, that I would be expelled from the country along with my sisters and parents, that I would bring failure and embarrassment to my whole family. When my Cockney/West London/NigEnglish accent failed, I reverted to my natural way of pronunciation, sobbing as I spoke. When that didn't work, thinking actions would speak louder than words, I begged in the traditional Nigerian way reserved for elders; I lay face down flat on the cold road of Notting Hill Gate, in broad daylight, grasped the policeman's boot and begged for leniency. He never budged. The policeman wrote my name, said he'd be watching me, and left.

Years later, I'd apply for a Criminal Records Bureau check, half frightened it would uncover my secret criminal life and I'd never be able to work with young people. I'd learn also the dark history the police have with men of colour, that there are far harsher encounters than mine. Some of us never breathe again. It would take the request for an essay, repeated visits to Notting Hill, an ascent and then a descent, to watch the ghost of my younger self rise, wondering what order and pronunciation of words would move men, how best the human body can convey meaning. I watch him brush dust and shame from his clothes and begin the silent and stumbling journey home.

THE SHARD

Joe Dunthorne

The setting sun picked out trees on the shore. Highland cows flicked their fringes in golden light. I watched the moon rise from the marshland, pouring silver into the lake. There is nothing more lethal to creativity than a beautiful view. I was at a desk in a room overlooking Loch Long, completely unable to write.

But luckily for me, our nation's nuclear defence came to the rescue. Trident submarine slid through the water with tugboats at its flanks and speedboats front and back, cruising at the speed of a funeral cortege. I had time to take in its radar-absorbent paint, a reflection-less black. I walked down to the shore and from there, saw the military base further down the loch, a brutal concrete bunker scooped out of the hillside. When I went back to my desk, I was ready to begin.

The view from my flat in London was never at risk of being *too beautiful* but, for a long time, it lacked any similarly motivating conflict. Imagine my relief when the Qatari government built The Shard. For my taste, skyscrapers should always resemble harbingers of a dark and hopeless future and, in this way, The Shard is honest, looking as it does like the eye of Sauron's tower, Mordor via Bank. Although one can't help feel that it still falls well short of the standard set by the world's largest and evilest skyscraper: the Burj Khalifa, Dubai. Nearly a thousand metres high, the Burj resembles the telescoping proboscis of some bombproof, planet-sized death beetle. It injects the skyline with terror. I have stood beneath it and can confirm that even the act of looking up at its highest point receives an appropriate punishment. *Suffer neck pain as you gaze upon me, mortal! Feel the spins as you struggle to focus on my impossibly-priced penthouses!* The Burj is so tall as to be clear of any stability-providing context, so that when you look up, it always seems to be falling, promising to destroy a mile-long knife-shaped stretch of the city. And The Burj is not just visually evil. It was built by ten thousand immigrant workers, mostly from India, Bangladesh and Pakistan. Many had their passports withheld until they'd earned enough to pay back the costs of flights and visas. That took a while since unskilled labourers got the equivalent of three pounds a day, and skilled labourers, a fiver. Now the building is built, tickets for a visit to the observation deck cost between twenty and seventy pounds. Officially, only one person died during construction (suicide) but, according to Human Rights Watch, other reasonable estimates put that number in the hundreds. Cue maniacal laughter.

Compared to the Burj, then, The Shard is little more than a minion, a henchman. In fact, since the arrival of 20 Fenchurch Street — "the walkie-talkie" — it may not even be the most evil skyscraper in London. The walkie-talkie boasts its own deathray. Last September, the concave glass near its summit redirected and magnified the sun's rays onto a stretch of Eastcheap, frying a Jaguar XJ and burning the hair on the heads of TV crews as they cooked eggs on the pavement. It now has malevolent nicknames: The Fryscraper, Walkie-Scorchie.

In fairness, it is difficult to imagine an official name more threatening than The Shard. The Shiv, perhaps. And The Shard is also the first and only building to obscure sightlines of St Paul's. For generations, city planners protected views of the cathedral but now, when seen from Primrose Hill, The Shard bursts through the side of the dome like a spear through a centurion's skull. Where the blitz missed, The Shard was on target.

In the streets around London Bridge, there are adverts for "Shangri-La Hotel at The Shard." (Why be in a building, when you could be at one?) Shangri-La refers to the 1933 novel, *Lost Horizon*, by James Hilton. In the book, a plane containing four Brits crash lands into an inaccessible Himalayan valley. There they find Shangri-La, a near-paradise that exists in the shadow of a 'gleaming pyramid...the loveliest mountain on earth... simple in outline as if a child had drawn it, and impossible to classify as to size, height or nearness.' There they meet mystical lamas who dedicate themselves 'to contemplation and to the pursuit of wisdom.'

Shangri-La Hotel, with The Shard as its mountain, dedicates itself to the pursuit of something more tangible, though no less exclusive. On the windows it says: "Opening Quarter Four". This is not a hotel for those who still cling to the sentimental comforts of the calendar months. If you live a life ruled by spring, summer, autumn and winter then clearly you lack the requisite trans-hemispherical holiday homes. The super-rich, freed from the tyranny of the seasons, will eat their blowtorched yellowfin while, half a mile below, we live-in tourists will be cooked alive by a deathray in the street.

I have long suspected that Zone One is the codename for a spaceship that — once it has successfully ejected all poor people from within its boundaries — will take off from the rest of the city. It will float above us, anchored to The Shard. When the weather is bad, it will simply rise up above the cloud line, angle itself towards the heat source and bathe. During especially vicious cold snaps, they can take Zone One for a weekend break, tether it to the Burj Khalifa. Every now and then, those of us still in the secondary boroughs will see a flock of used copies of *How To Spend It* falling from the sky. They will also send down their gamey turds to help manure the perma-shaded land on which nothing will grow. On the day the Thames flood barrier gives way, the citizens of Zone One will take to their balconies and bask in nature's spectacle.

On the day I went up The Shard, it seemed that I was in fact witnessing the spacecraft making its ascent. London had disappeared. There was thick smoke or was it cloud, I could not say. But then the weather cleared and the city materialized again.

"What's that tiny thing that looks like St Paul's?" I said.

It was St Paul's.

Trains slithered in and out of London Bridge. Tugs dragged rafts of freight containers down the dishwatery Thames. A plane took off from City Airport, pitching steeply up to clear Canary Wharf. From here, London's second tallest building — One Canada Square — looked laughably benign. The biggest revelation was that the buses were not *red on top*. Apparently it helps keep them cool in summer. Not that there will be any sunshine once the spaceship blocks the sky.

I looked for somewhere to sit and take notes. I searched the viewing platform but found nowhere to perch. It took me a while to understand that this was policy.

"Enjoying 'The View'?" a young team member asked me, visibly dying. All staff had been trained to offer infantilising small talk.

I asked if there was anywhere up here I could get a cup of tea, sit down, I was even willing to pay. There were restaurants, she said, but I could not access them. I would have to go down two lifts, out of the building, walk around the block, and come in the other side, with the residents. The architects had been careful to separate those who can only afford to *look* at The View from those who can afford to own it.

It was almost dark by the time I got home. From my desk, it was reassuring to look out at The Shard and know that its atmosphere of evil was not just skin-deep. As I watched it, four red lights blinked on, positioned like ostentatious buttons, running from its base to its peak. Officially they were there to warn aircraft but I recognised them as standby lights for a bigger project. On the day those reds turn green, Zone One will shrug itself free of the forgettable boroughs, the changeable weather, and take its rightful place in the sun.

STAVE HILL

Tom Chivers

This *has* to be the flattest place in London. Rotherhithe: a land without hills, without towers. As we set out, Sarah and I, following the subtlest gradient of Salter Road, I spot one lone apartment block and a disused gas cylinder — its rings like a skeletal ribcage — edging the sky. But their effect is merely to reinforce the uncanny level of this place; its diffuse architecture of low-rise new-builds and scrappy hedges. The only people out walking are accompanied by dogs. Bulldogs, terriers, snub-nosed Staffies straining at their leashes. We are crunching curling leaves underfoot. I will never understand the logic of keeping a pet that must be muzzled.

Geologically speaking, the entire Rotherhithe peninsula overlays a band of alluvial silt deposited by the meandering Thames in an age before embankments and flood defences. By right, it is more a part of the river than it is the dry land. The affinities of Rotherhithe's landscape and people with water are as deep and varied as the soapy back-wash of the river itself. Before the construction of flood walls, the Thames would have washed the land at high tide, leaving an environment of sodden marshes riddled with tidal creeks. Occasionally the remains of wooden causeways — prehistoric routes across the badlands — are dredged from building sites. Later, dykes and drainage channels were cut to make the land serviceable as pasture, and the shifting shoreline formalised by earth banks and wooden revetments. By the seventeenth century the entire riverfront from Bermondsey to Greenwich was teeming with wharfs, jetties and dockyards to service the growing trade hub of London. And it was from Rotherhithe, in July 1620, that an ageing cargo ship (or *fluyt*) called The Mayflower set sail for the New World.

We have been living here for one month, in a place most Londoners have barely heard of. The wind is harsh, and after dusk, when I make the ten minute walk from the Tube station, the streets are eerily quiet. An evening jogger, locked in to their playlist. A bird breaking the dark skin of Surrey Water. It's a far cry from our nine years living above the raucous hustlers of Petticoat Lane Market. And where the East End is the site of arrival for immigrants seeking a better life in the city, Rotherhithe is a place of departures, a place of endings. The Pilgrim Fathers setting out for the coast of Massachusetts. Swift's Gulliver leaving home for the South Seas. And when ships do return to Rotherhithe, it is usually to die. Ship-breaking was a major industry here: vessels reduced to their component parts, sold for scrap, left to rot on the foreshore like the carcasses of whales.

A peninsula is a dead end. Take the single-decker C10 from Bermondsey and see how quickly the city thins out the further in you get: the solid, busy matter of streets and offices and people dissipates along the snaking path of Rotherhithe Street. It's impossible to believe there is anything further east until the bus shifts back onto the Lower Road to Deptford. Visually, Rotherhithe is caught between The Shard to the west and, across the bend in the river to the east, the looming pyramids of Canary Wharf. This alignment with the city's two highest points serves only to strengthen our sense of the peninsula as flatland, an urban *tabula rasa*.

With no hills of its own, the only option for Rotherhithe

was to build one. From the tip of the peninsula — its most northern point — we turn off the main road and head south into the heart of the peninsula, passing first Mellish Sports Ground and then Bacon's College — alma mater of boxer David Haye and *Big Brother* contestant Jade Goody. Lagado Mews becomes Timber Pond Road. The atmospherics of the Rotherhithe interior are so uniformly suburban we could be in the outskirts of any small town in the south of England. Only the sporadic sight of the Gherkin or One Canada Square peeping over a retaining wall or emerging at distance through plane trees reminds us where we are. Reaching the suggestively-named Dock Hill Avenue, we see the Hill for the first time, at the apex of a dead-straight, tree-lined footpath, its perfect symmetry framed by a sky now wiped clean of cloud.

Stave Hill is a thirty feet-high grass mound in the shape of a truncated cone (or *frustrum*). Its form is suggestive of the Command Module of a space rocket that, having re-entered the earth's atmosphere, has crash-landed unnoticed in SE16. A local boy, awake in the wee hours, might have heard the collision; perhaps even, half-dreaming, seen the outline of a body rustling the bushes by the wheelie bins: Rotherhithe's own Extra Terrestrial.

To climb this Hill is to participate in a ritual ascension. The approach seems designed to echo the geometric avenues of Avebury; a sloping path marked at regular intervals by large rectangular structures swamped in ivy — ruined municipal megaliths that loom above the joggers and dog walkers. The Hill itself is a kind of miniature of the prehistoric chalk mound at Silbury, Wiltshire. The grass is luminous, as if it has been dowsed in glow-in-the-dark green paint. I almost expect Bilbo Baggins — or the Teletubbies — to emerge from a trapdoor in its flank.

Stave Hill's skin may be turfy, but its innards are all rubble and waste. Just like the mounds of Arnold Circus (2.3 miles north-west) and Northala Fields (14.5 miles north-west by west), the Hill is a glorified slag heap; constructed in 1985 using the spoil from the dismantling of Stave and Russia Docks. As we ascend the concrete stairway that reaches up the face of the mound in the manner of a Mayan pyramid, I am thinking of a set of black and white photographs of the Surrey Docks taken by my friend Bill Pearson in the early 1980s.[1] A Cumbrian émigré, Bill ended up in south-east London and became a compulsive walker and chronicler of an industrial landscape on the cusp of ruin and renewal. In one photograph, local children are swimming in an abandoned dock basin, metres from a curdled mass of floating junk. In another, a grotesque still life, what looks like the disarticulated bow of a cargo barge lies tits-up on an empty dockside, with two stilled rig cranes for company.

Stave Hill is a memorial to this disappeared world. It is also, quite literally, *made of it*. Perhaps, then, it is more like a cairn: a gathering of local materials into a waymarker or ritual node. Nothing new. Nothing alien. Nothing that cannot be collected from the immediate environment and redeployed. Stave Hill is as good a symbol of London than any: an entire city built on the accumulated rubble of its past.

The summit of the Hill is flat, concrete and wind-blown. The views over the city are staggering. I survey the skyscrapers of the Square Mile several miles away to the north-west, The Shard stabbing

---

[1] Bill Pearson, 'Two Men and a Dog' in *The London Column*, 30th August 2013 (http://thelondoncolumn.com/2013/08/30/two-men-and-a-dog).

knife-like into the sky. The turrets of Tower Bridge and the London Eye are like children's toys, absurdly miniature. The towers of Canary Wharf rise up in front of us so close you feel you could reach right in. I look back across South Bermondsey and Peckham past the ridge of hills where I grew up, to where the television transmitter stands on the ruins of the Crystal Palace. I spot the square tower of St Anne's Church rising above the riverfront buildings of Limehouse. And due west, past Strata SE1 at the Elephant and Castle, I make out St George's Wharf Tower, Vauxhall in the hazy distance. Oddly, the only major feature we cannot see is the Thames herself, obscured by all the buildings hustling in on her banks. Great slug of river. *Strong brown god.*[2]

The shouts of Sunday League footballers carry on the wind from the sports ground. Birdsong from the Stave Hill Ecological Park, a necklace of urban woodland encircling the base of the mound. A plane soars into the heavens from City Airport.

Stave Hill is a promontory from which, above all, you look not down but up; up towards One Canada Square, the eight hundred-foot tower at the heart of Canary Wharf. London's Science Fiction reality. In the Sci-Fi horror film 28 Weeks Later (2007), the Isle of Dogs is depicted as a fortified safe zone from which to begin the repopulation of Britain after a zombie apocalypse. At the start of the film US military snipers patrol the rooftops of Docklands, but when it all goes horribly wrong we end up, inevitably, in an abandoned Tube tunnel. For a moment, it is all utterly believable. What goes up must — you know — come down. Stave Hill is not a peak to

---

[2] T.S. Eliot, *The Four Quartets*, Harcourt (1943). Eliot's direct referent is the Ganges, but the Thames is felt as a sustained echo in his poem.

be conquered, but a viewing platform for the vertical city that is happening elsewhere.

We are joined on the summit by a thirty-something man wearing jogging bottoms and a grey Hooters tank top. (The back carries the company slogan: 'Delightfully tacky, yet unrefined'.) He has a shaven head, carries a small towel, and sports the frame of a man who spends more time in the gym than is healthy. Two minutes later — as we are busy studying a scale model of the Surrey Docks that is, appropriately, half-filled with rainwater — another man joins him. He is panting and wearing more Lycra than is healthy. With his arty spectacles and designer stubble, he could be a media analyst or a trader. They set about using the railings at the top of the Hill to perform squats. Before too long they are sprinting up and down the steps, each time the second man letting out a more pained gasp than the last as he reaches the top.

In recent years Stave Hill has become a magnet for fitness enthusiasts; a kind of outdoor gymnasium for personal trainers and companies like Breathe Fitness, Wild Forest Gym and Bootcamp SE16. The latter maintains a lively Twitter feed, recording the exploits of its participants in tendon-crunching detail — from 'strength circuits' and 'endurance drills to improve cardio levels' to 'single leg tyre squats for ultimate glute and core strength' and 'crab crawls up Stave Hill'.

Beneath the skin of this place lies a forgotten history of labour — of stevedores and deal porters testing their strength and skill against steel and timber. But in Stave Hill the ruins of their yards are refashioned as a recreational treadmill; the same territories reworked by the twenty-first century leisure-seeker in engineered sportswear and tracking his progress via a fitness app on his smartphone. The body, he proposes, may have topography too. Sculpt me a landscape of undulating pecs and quads. Level the surplus; pump up the rest.

We descend the mound and head north, following a footpath deep into the Ecological Park, tracing the sunken line of an old dock channel, now brimming with dense foliage and infrequent bursts of colour where the Council has planted something exotic. A girl in Ugg boots passes by with a scruffy dog. Two Eastern Europeans smoking roll-ups. A young man with his arm in a sling and a pit bull the colour of sand. It is a manufactured wildness that has reclaimed the old docks, but it will do. Who knows the day when the tide will break in, to take back the flatlands? You will find us high up, close to the sky.

BATTERSEA POWER STATION

Bradley L. Garrett

T he snaking shuffle of the train from Platform 12 at Clapham Junction to Victoria always seems more of a meander than other rail connections. The rhythmic, side-to-side bounce lulls passengers into stillness, suspended a single story over the bustle of south London chippies and chicken joints. Pausing briefly at Battersea Park Station, pressing one's head against the breathy window condensation with eye-cupped hands provides a rare back-glimpse. A slow turn bends the carriages to reveal the moving body from inside its centripetal shell. There, hundreds of strangers swipe at screens and skim sections of free newspapers: routine distractions.

Crossing the carriage in a surfing shamble as the train regains its speed toward Victoria, our final destination, the view from the window on the right hand side is engulfed by a fifty thousand cubic metre, powder-blue gasometer. Inevitably, when the gasholder moves aside, as if being wheeled off set, the hulking expanse of Battersea Power Station (A Side) slides into frame with sleek force. Many of the daily papers are then subtly laid on laps and devices coyly raised to capture. A multitude of eyes flit across millions of bricks, hundreds of blown-out windows and four creamy smokestacks, impossibly small gulls drifting amongst it all, squawking information to each other about air currents and vulnerable river creatures ripe for plucking with a swift nosedive from the derelict industrial cranes perched over the south bank of the Thames. The historical imagination thus springs into life — a movement through time with a suggestive vertical stretch, from chimney rim to tidal rip. And deeper. Steam and smoke and energy didn't just get pumped into the 20th century industrial airborne quagmire through those slick stacks; it was also driven into dripping and calcifying tunnels, under the Thames, to the north bank, heating council flats in Pimlico.

Focusing on the windows or bricks of the building, or even its infrastructural nether-regions, opens up all sorts of imaginative spaces, but it's really the chimneys I've always been in love with, jutting as they do into the slow clouds at their own indolent pace, oblivious but somehow smug. Overwhelmed by a desire to touch them, a friend and I wiggled through a broken wooden slat under the raised railway on 5th November and ran across the property in a euphoric panic well-suited to Bonfire Night. After squeezing under some loose fencing, climbing the decaying girders buttressing the brick and up onto the scaffolding hedging the base of the stacks, we finally made it a quarter of the way up the northwest chimney of A Side. Perched on janky scaffold planks, I turned the lid on a bottle of whiskey past the safety clicks. I drank deeply as the explosions began in Battersea Park and reclined against the taupe-toned concrete, caressing its texture while tiny fragments crumbled inside, dislodged by bursts of colour, the din of human screams in the park below accentuating our vertical isolation. My sense of fulfilment was far more intoxicating than the whiskey or rockets.

Back on the rails again days later, I'm even more attentive whilst riding the gleaming tracks that converge on Victoria, skirting the borders of the power station, as if the building has leprosy, a rotting London limb every developer is sure will crumble any day now. Yet it's not hard to imagine the chimneys vivaciously smoking, after touching them while they were rhythmically crumbling on Bonfire Night. Pasted to the window as we rapidly approach the swirling river again, sharing the transient trance with like-minded passengers enraptured by the decaying husk, I try to unfocus my eyes using a technique developed glaring at those dot drawings from the 1990s one could coax mammal shapes from, sold at immobile wheeled wagons in the middle of shopping malls. That cross-eyed sensation reminds me of a late-night retina flicker MDMA comedown and my heart races. Vision thus blurred, I can almost get the chimneys chugging again as my jowls slacken in the effort to visually pull back, blood pumping in my ears.

Bringing the power station back into focus, I imagine pushing on the side of it and watching the roots of the building springing and ripping out of the ground, buried pipes and cables snapping and spurting, upturning million-year-old rocks covered in shit-stinking silt, Roman skulls rolling into the Thames with coins in their eyes, plunging into the wrong waterway two thousand years late. The station, rolled over entirely now, standing on its four skinny legs (which I'm sure could work), is finally ready to walk away from its island of excommunication, wobbling west to Surbiton or Moseley to resettle into a less pressured riverfront space.

However, it's not just the 'land' developers want; it's the possibility of getting sewn into all that connective urban tissue. If you were to take a large, hot knife and slide it through London, insert thumbs and slowly peel it apart into two halves, it would become clear the city exceeds it horizontal expanse in profile. Below us, hidden rivers and sewers, cable conduits, road and utility tunnels, trains tubes, deep shelters and government citadels are hemmed in by disused, dysfunctional and forgotten features, Victorian vaults of ingenuity and ambition. Underneath this snarl thousand-tonne tunnel-boring machines with names like 'Phyllis' and 'Sophia', Brunel's mutant offspring, are ripping through bedrock at a forty-metre depth, inches at a time, a cyborg earthworm ingesting ancient urban underbelly, shitting it out in piles to be dumped on Wallasea Island in Essex where birds will nest in pulverised Palaeozoic London fossils, spied on by birders from London who have travelled to Essex to see 'nature'. Because of all this frantic digging, every once in a while, laser sensors placed strategically around London set off alarms because an induced tectonic slippage slumped part of the architectural horizon.

From street level up, the London skyline is equally vast, a traversable range of peaks and plateaus. From windy, often wet, heights, you experience the age-old sensation of always thinking the next peak will be slightly higher, provide a slightly better vantage point, as we race against the architectural subsidence and formation of new points of the horizon — like the aptly named Pinnacle building. Thus the quest begins: the negotiation for spatial access, wiggling up drainpipes, throwing climbing slings tied to tennis balls over fire escapes just out of reach, borrowing cleaning staff keys from carts parked in quiet hotel corridors, chatting up concierges and climbing cold construction site scaffolding toward clouds reflecting the twinkle of the metropolis. Each ascent provides a satisfaction that lasts just long enough to sharply inhale the eye-watering London miasma, shaving a few days off your life and a few percentage points off your lung capacity, before eyeing up another prime suspect for top view and starting all over again. When, on rare occasions, a particular summit satisfies the yearning for more than a few days, the pull to return becomes irresistible and a love affair with a building begins to occlude everything else, resigning everyday life to the margins of interest. My affair with Battersea, thus situated, is lusty and hot after our last tryst and I want more.

A few weeks after that first ascent, I received a text message from a friend with a photo of the same chimney we had climbed from the opposite one, on the southwest corner of A Side. In it, an imperceptible figure in black was hanging from the side of the stack, suspended by an invisible rope, far above the top of the scaffolding from which I had watched the fireworks. The photo induced feral impulses in me and the next time I slinked by on the train, I began to weep. A man next to me, in a cheap Marks and Spencer suit, with dead, dark, weight under his eyes and an egg sandwich and crisps in a rumpled Tesco carrier bag at his feet, looked toward me and we briefly made eye contact. His initial shock and embarrassment slowly turned into a downward smile and squint of admiration stained with sadness, an acknowledgment that he too was overwhelmed. As we turned back to the windows, I saw him involuntarily shiver in my peripheral vision before I began doing my MDMA eye trick on the architecture again.

The next time we ran across the derelict perimeter into the power station, through the no-man's land of Japanese knotweed, ancient industrial rubble, hard-packed repatriated soil and now, hulking construction equipment ripping up the yard, our comparatively tiny frames were saddled with climbing equipment. We negotiated some noisy temporary fencing, and made it to the base of the building. My friend scaled the decaying internal girders and dropped down a hauling rope. I attached fifty kilos of kit. I was sure security was sitting somewhere, listening to the all-too-human tugging sounds, deploying an intruder 'action plan'. But they never arrived, so I followed the bags up. Past the rooftop, at the top of the scaffolding again, with one gloved hand on the cold concrete of the stack, connected to an infinitesimal white rope dangling in the frigid wind by a couple of metal ascenders and a harness, I stuck my foot in a loop and lifted off. Metre by metre, crunching, pushing, pulling, standing, grunting, resting and repeating, I made it to the top and pulled myself up to stand on the lip of the chimney.

There, I looked down at a temporary white tent in the middle of the power station, placed there by an ambitious developer who may have an analogous affinity for the place, and considered the inevitable dismemberment of this pained little piece of land I've come to love so much. The chimney that will replace the one I'm standing on, a simulacrum of its former self, with a one hundred and ten-metre public viewing platform, will be stripped of certain essences. For instance: the pink pig that detached itself from the stacks, floating into the Heathrow flight path in 1967, will never have been attached to those replacement casts. Nor will we. Nor will they crumble in the same tantalising way every Bonfire Night.

An acquired British sociality for embarrassment of nostalgia pulls me from my reverie and I climb down, putting my weight on the rope again. I'm back in my body, with an unbearable tension in my arms as I dangle just under the pinnacle of the stack, somehow unable to let go and push the handle on my descender to get back to the scaffold planking. I'm locked in a permanent gripping muscle suspension that, whilst perhaps relaying an air of stasis to a downlooker (what would this situation look like from a low-flying plane?), is actually surging through me in powerful waves. Hovering in the cold, strung up by pieces of metal pressed from a machine in Taiwan that passed through the hands of people I'll never meet, attached to an anchor sunk by a power station worker from my grandparents' generation who clearly had faith in the metal, the concrete, to hold their weight, threaded into fabric easily sliced with a sharp blade, staring over a sea of lights and a rush of muddy water that looks blue, painted by those lights, the soft sound of the train, my train, slithering and shaking its way around the perimeter of the island, involuntarily discharging metal-on-metal showers of midnight sparks and high-pitched shrieks, I let my hands slip off the rope. The fleeting arthritis of cold and fear that gripped me slinks through, down the ridges of the chimney and into the ground, though the tunnels, into the water table. I'm limp, suspended, satiated.

BLACKHEATH

Chrissy Williams

I am in search of *blauegris* on top of Blackheath. I burn my boat at the station and turn to Lewisham Hill.

Two men spray a car with high-pressure jets under the railway bridge, water droplets rebounding across sunlight, out onto the pavement through bright blue iron railings. Overhead the sky is a solid grey and stray raindrops fall. Small patches of blue wait their turns on the sidelines, glimpsed briefly between houses and the arches. On the other side of the road a Private Shop has its windows blacked out, denying light all together, although a hand-written sign on the front door shows a friendly intention: OPEN!

Lewisham Hill curls into a residential street, an incongruous mix of Victorian terraces, 1930s flats and post-war purpose-built housing. The road is a long straight tree trunk pressed flat into the hill, rising gently, narrower streets branching off and skirting round the hillside. Cats peer out of wide windows, the houses' only visible inhabitants. It is a world of cats.

The wind pushes south-east, upwards. The wind pushes everything upwards, including the huge trees lining the pavement every ten steps or so, which seem to lean and point up towards the heath, along with the ivy and shrubs all tilting in the same direction. No *blauegris* though, not yet.

One of the Victorian houses is built around a strange square tower. Each of its windows has been renovated in isolation from the others, a mixture of sash, Victorian arch and 1980s flat plaster. How does the window change the view? The top of the tower has three full sash windows on each side of it. The view from that twelve-windowed room must be back over Bermondsey, back over the river into central London. The view across the street is of a dilapidated block of 1930s flats called *The Hermitage*. "It's better to live in the shit house than the nice house," said my friend once, "because then at least you have a view of the nice house."

Looking up the gradual slope of speed-bumps and bus stops, a small triangular patch of rough grass appears from nowhere on the right. There is a low-cut tree stump on the edge of it in the process of being reclaimed by long grass. The pavement stops and turns into a path here, a muddy pathway flattening the grasses, steepening up around to the right. This must be the beginning of the heath.

Directly ahead, on the park's left-hand edge, is an eight-foot red brick wall which surrounds a mess of 1960s apartments in three or four different blocks. Someone has painted a large white stag on the heavy dark wooden door in the middle of the wall. There is faded illegible graffiti on the bricks next to it. The stag has not been allowed to fade. It is a marker. A welcome.

Up around the corner now the ground flattens and looks outward to a larger area of open land. Is this the whole heath now? It's still tiny. Can this be it?

There is a large, red-brick house in the centre of the foreground, its trees, garden and outhouses obstructing a wider view of the heath, hiding behind bars. We need to get around it. The sign on the open gate says it is an army cadet training centre. A couple appear from behind it with two dogs: a lolling golden retriever prances straight into the training grounds while a stern tan dachshund runs to the gates and barks at him. The walkers shout out an unintelligible name in high pitch, and the larger dog returns to an immediate leash. The smaller dog is rewarded for its restraint with a few paces' more freedom.

On the other side of the training centre grounds, Blackheath reveals itself more completely: a wide open space that stretches far into the distance. Look at the flatness, the unwieldy sprawl of the grassy plateau. There don't seem to be any shrubs in the vicinity though, no *blauegris*. Houses are behind us, but far ahead there are further rows of trees, further possible houses, possible spires. There are gentle undulations but no peak in sight. The grasses roll on.

As the rough field extends away in an unmanageable shape, a long thin road breaks into it, cutting off a triangular wedge. Occasional cars move slowly along it. All the cars are completely, suspiciously silent.

A commercial plane begins to growl overhead, slow and low, and it is all that can be heard over the invisible wind which is still rushing fiercely up from the hill road behind us, drowning out any noise on the heath and blowing it away, pushing it out into the centre of the park. The absence of road noise renders the traffic an unreal presence against the giant roar of the open sky. The plane passes. The rumble dissipates. A single-deck red bus crosses nearby with a familiar, audible sigh, the soothing switch into a lower register as it moves from right to left across our field of view.

You could be forgiven for losing your sense of direction in an open space like this, on such a cloudy day, with so little noise to give context. The grass extends in every direction. It is like swimming in deep water.

Canary Wharf's familiar beacon suddenly peers out from the treeline on the left. Moving onwards The Shard reveals itself too, appearing from a tall townhouse behind us, another waypoint from which we take our bearings. The Great Bear. The Gawdy Shard. The Wharf Which Flashes Even By Daylight.

They are all so far away though. Look back across the heath. There is nothing but empty disappointment here on this strange even lattice of land.

Crossing onto the next triangular wedge, a flock of perhaps thirty small seagulls sit on the grass like ducks. Occasionally one gets up and leans into the strong wind which lifts it up and floats it over the head of another gull, letting it land and settle down in front of it. How wonderful it must be to fly.

An empty beer can rolls in front of the flock, left last night perhaps. How eerie it is up here alone in the dark, with the wind and the roaring sky and the stars falling back into infinity. Each narrow street is punctuated with lampposts, thin black poles which offer little consolation against the darkness. I remember reading that Blackheath was once planted with gibbets, "on which the bleaching bones of men who dared to ask for some extension of liberty were left year after year to dangle in the wind." In place of each streetlight imagine an execution. In place of each dark beam that blinks, imagine a death.

Into the next wedge now and — *is the ground raised slightly here?* — the grass clumps into thicker patches, and the blades are longer, wider, more like fingers. The wind runs over and through them, setting them in motion like wind-pushed wavelets that ripple across the barrelling bodies of larger waves. The sea here is green. The birds settle in it.

There is some kind of raised area here though: a shrubbery, some small trees. Perhaps this is the highest point of the plateau?

Trying to understand what the greenery hides, moving towards it we see a pond running its own rigid ripples across the surface, the wind blowing so hard it looks like it's at a slant.

Benches positioned around the pond are the only thing which suggest it was not a result of recent flooding. It is shallow, a pocket of the heath which might have collected rainwater instead of soaking it into the earth, a shabby mistake of thick mud and grass. There is a red flag on the far side which looks as though it has been planted by a diver to mark out a channel. Getting closer, it is in fact an umbrella blown inside out — a red umbrella with the canvas detached from its broken frame, the rounded wooden handle barely visible beneath the surface of the dull, dark water. Maybe it is a marker too. Maybe it marks something temporary, ephemeral, out here in all this space.

Moving onwards the park fans out further, even further than was visible before, and in different directions. It's so broad and flat, and the sky so agitated, you can see the shadows of clouds running across the grass, individual grasses glistening in turn. You can feel the different thicknesses, the densities of each cloud on your shoulders as they pass overhead. A single flash of sunlight warms your body in divine light, gone in an instant. Here at the bottom of the sky, in the open geometric heathland, you are exposed.

An awkward white line stains the grass underfoot and, looking up, it stretches out across the park into a sports field. In the summer each segment of this place must be taken over by lobster bodies worshipping the sun, kite-flyers, picnic-goers, donkey-riders, the donkeys themselves jerking at flies, spending each day walking slowly in one direction, and then slowly back again. But in the winter now it's empty. Strip away the people and the sun and the houses and all you have is an empty expanse, in the city but not of it.

I brought you here in search of *blauegris*. I recall now the name came from a dream. Blackheath's first recorded name is *Blachehedfel* and I must have transformed it in my sleep, skewing language into a single living plant which I might find and pluck out, be free to take home with me. But there is no *blauegris* here any more than there is a summit, any more than there is any single place on this heath where a person could sit and feel satisfied that they had reached their journey's end, had reached any kind of resolution.

The first settlers who came here along the river burnt their boat upon arrival. I never stray further from a bus stop than a ten-minute walk. In the absence of neat conclusions, continue.

We need to get to the bus stop now. This wind is so cold. We need to cross this new road that has even more traffic moving along it. The cars are heavy and loud and they will not stop for us. The nearest crossing is a distant walk away and it will be disappointing to find in the final moments that we are obliged to follow a single prescribed human route across this open plain.

Take my hand.

Perhaps we can lean into the strong wind and let it lift us up and float over the heads of the cars, let it land us and settle us softly on the other side.

Perhaps we can lift our heads and look up into the sky, up into the perfect unbroken view of the sky which is Blackheath's gift. Look out with me past the city, which we leave noiseless behind us, past the towers and the clouds, past the atmosphere and into the dark, endless night beyond, all the stars rushing to meet us in a frenzy.

Let go of my hand now and experience this alone.

TELEGRAPH HILL

David Cooper

I have never lived in London. For a few years, though, my working weeks began on the West Coast Main Line as I travelled down from the Lake District — where I was based at the Wordsworth Trust in Grasmere — to spend sun-deprived hours in subterranean research libraries and archives in the capital. It was a life of pleasingly polarised geographies. I woke up, on Monday mornings, to the screeches of the Canadian geese over the northern end of the lake at Grasmere; then, a few hours later, I experienced auditory overload when stepping out onto Euston Road. The juxtapositions continued in London itself: days were spent in darkened rooms researching minor works by neglected Picturesque landscape painters; and evenings unfolded in the phosphorous glow of the turn-of-the-millennium city. My experience of London was also defined by a narrowly circumscribed and centralised geography as I rarely moved outside a quadrant which contained Tate Britain in the west and the Courtauld Institute in the east, the British Library in the north and the Royal Watercolour Society on the south bank. As a result, my sense of the city's verticality was exclusively shaped by architectural thrusts upwards: the 1960s glass of Millbank Tower, for instance, which, at the time, served as New Labour HQ; and the functional brickwork of Gilbert Scott's Bankside Power Station which had recently been Tate-ified amidst the glow of Blairite largesse. It was a sense of constructed verticality which was reinforced by the fin-de-siècle fantasies of the starchitects whose CAD-facilitated imaginings were rapidly reshaping the city's skyline. I looked skywards as the Gherkin came into being and predicted, with justifiable confidence, what Wordsworth would have made of the ever-evolving view of St Paul's from Westminster Bridge.

By extension, London's outer boroughs remained unvisited, to borrow a cardinal Wordsworthian term, and purely toponymical. My knowledge of the city's outlying topography was thin: a figurative conflation of what the contemporary edgelands poet, Paul Farley, describes as 'the slow outskirts' glimpsed as the train crawled into Euston and an imagined geography shaped by Wordsworth's idealised vision of the city radiating out from Westminster Bridge 'Open to the fields, and to the sky,/ All bright and glittering in the smokeless air'. London for me, then, was not a city of naturally high places. Instead, natural elevation was indelibly associated in my mind with the contours of Loughrigg and Silver Howe, Helm Crag and Seat Sandal, back home at Grasmere: fells which I continued to encounter daily, even in London, through the late eighteenth-century brushstrokes of the artists — such as Francis Towne and John 'Warwick' Smith — I found myself researching in those darkened interiors.

This centrifugal sense of urban space contrasted with my parents' experiences of London. My Mum and Dad spent much of their twenties living in various boroughs both north and south of the river. London, for them, was defined by the centripetality characteristic of the practice of everyday life in the city; and, in terms of embodied experience, they were more familiar with the streets of Highbury and Hackney than the over-determined spaces of the post-imperial centre. For several years after their marriage, they lived in a ground-floor flat on Erlanger Road in New Cross, just around the corner from Goldsmith's College. Unsurprisingly, then, a favourite location for my newly-wed parents was Telegraph Hill: a place-name which played an improbably prominent role in shaping my own imagining of London when I was brought up, some years later, under the not-always-so-grey suburban skies of south Liverpool. Walking uphill was a quotidian practice for my Mum and Dad in south-east London; Telegraph Hill's natural contours allowed them to see, from a distance, the manmade elevations of central London.

As local historian, John Kelly, points out in a pamphlet published by the Telegraph Hill Society, this elevated land — to the south of the hamlet of Hatcham — was known, up until the end of the eighteenth century, as Plow'd Garlick Hill: a pleasingly poetic place-name which carries a sense of the historic rurality of this terrain which now falls in the Borough of Lewisham.[1] Chaucer's 'nyne and twenty' pilgrims would have passed close to this mound as they walked — imaginatively, at least — from Southwark to Canterbury. For the most part, though, the history of the hill — which rises to just under fifty metres above sea level — seems to have been uneventfully agricultural. In 1795, however, the Admiralty responded to the threat of a French invasion by establishing an optical telegraph station at the summit of this gentle incline. As Kelly explains, the Admiralty advanced beyond the lit beacon as a mode of communication by installing a shutter telegraph: a contraption which was approximately

---

[1] I would like to express my gratitude to Malcolm Bacchus, Chair of the Telegraph Hill Society, for generously sending me a copy of John Kelly's pamphlet on 'The Telegraph on Telegraph Hill'.

twenty feet high and which contained 'six wooden shutters, arranged as two side-by-side sets each three shutters high'. The innovative optical technology — which, with rich irony, had first been developed by the Frenchman Claude Chappe — enabled the Admiralty to establish a direct line of communication linking Whitehall, West Square at Southwark, Shooter's Hill and so on, until reaching the Kent coast at Deal. Through the installation of the technology of military communications, then, Plow'd Garlick Hill metamorphosed into Telegraph Hill. By extension, the hill emerged into the national consciousness when in 1815 it played a pivotal role in relaying news of Wellington's victory at Waterloo to Admiralty House. Telegraph Hill continued to function as a vital communication link over the course of the first half of the 19th century; and, as Kelly points out, the shutter system was superseded by more advanced semaphore technology. In 1847 the naval line was finally shut down; but in spite of the relative brevity of the existence of the telegraph station, its important history continues to be traced, of course, in the naming of this hill.

The landscape immediately on and around Telegraph Hill was radically transformed in the second half of the 19th century. During the 1840s, Robert Browning lived at Telegraph Cottage near New Cross Road in a local environment dominated by the Market Gardens of the Worshipful Company of Haberdashers. With the coming of the railways the Company identified the potential for significant property development and, in 1859, the surveyor William Snooke produced a detailed report recommending the laying of expansive tree-lined roads for the construction of 'dwelling houses of a high standard'. As a result, the 1870s saw the Haberdashers' Company lay out what was labelled Hatcham Manor Estate: a network of roads — including Erlanger, Pepys and Jermingham — featuring lines of substantial terrace houses situated on the slopes of the hill.

As a result, Telegraph Hill now came to be situated in prosperous suburbia and, through the creation of a public park (formally opened in April 1895) the highest point was retained as a much-desired green space for the residents of the sizeable new houses fanning out below. Telegraph Hill was reshaped into a site of leisure and pleasure. As Kelly helpfully explains, it is a transformation which is recorded by the splendidly sniffy Mrs Evelyn Cecil in *London Parks and Gardens* (1907) when she notes that: 'The site of the semaphore station is now a level green for lawn tennis. On the other side of the roadway, the descent is steep into the valley, and there are two small ponds at the bottom. The cliffs are covered in turf, interspersed by the usual meaningless clumps of bushes and a few nice trees.' Clearly, Cecil still pays attention to the natural contours of this raised ground. Crucially, though, the crest of the hill is immediately presented as a recreational zone for the ever-emerging middle classes residing on its slopes; an elevated location which proved ideal for a spot of tennis against a panoramic backdrop of the architectural skyline of central London.

On a Saturday afternoon in November 2013, I visited Telegraph Hill with my Dad. I had mapped it all out in my head beforehand: the coming together at Euston; the journey on the Tube to New Cross Gate; the visit to the corner-shop where my parents stopped off on their way home each evening; and the opportunity to peer into their old flat on Erlanger Road. Most of all, though, I was anticipating what Caroline Dale, in *Skyline London: A Guide to the Finest Views from the Capital's High Points* (2012), tantalisingly describes as 'a view of the entire canon of London's skyline signature buildings', including the vertical lines of Tate Modern and Millbank which I had only ever witnessed near-at-hand. A late November visit was promisingly timely since, as Dale suggests, the panoramic view of the cityscape from Telegraph Hill is 'at its best when the trees are not in leaf'.

Perhaps predictably, though, the view from the out-of-season tennis courts was disappointing. That Saturday, we were late getting away and, by the time we took the path through the small park, the afternoon greyness was beginning to converge with the early evening gloaming. The promised central London skyline, then, remained frustratingly out of sight as my Dad told me about a time-before-me and a life which he and my Mum shared but I will never be able to access fully. Intermittently, the geometry of the London skyline would reveal itself through the dullness: the vertical towers of Battersea Power Station; the high circle of the London Eye; and, in a not-entirely-harmonious bringing together of these shapes, the more recent form of Strata SE1 at Elephant and Castle. For the most part, however, the eye was drawn to the Whistleresque image of the aircraft warning lights on The Shard. That is to say, sharp red dots shone through the mizzle and reached us on our park bench on Telegraph Hill: a site which my parents had visited together on an almost daily basis over forty years earlier.

The visual spectacle afforded by the walk up Telegraph Hill was an anti-climax. It was a sense of disappointment demonstrably shared by the number of Goldsmith's students who were in the park that afternoon, equipped with digital cameras and mobile phones, and who had made the same journey up from New Cross Road in order to show off the vertical metropolis to their visiting parents. Yet even as we sat together on that park bench, it became clear that the smudged skyline was an entirely appropriate image for this exercise in memory capture. As we sat in Telegraph Hill Park, my Dad's thoughts inevitably remained transfixed on the contented summer of 1967 whilst my own mind drifted back to those days of scholarly excavation researching Lake District landscape paintings in central London. As we sat in Telegraph Hill Park, the imaginative presence of Wordsworth — the great poet of both high places and the difficult-to-grasp nature of memory — came back into view. Wordsworth's preoccupation with the naming of places prompted reflections on the military history of this elevated spot. I momentarily recalled how the Wordsworths famously celebrated the news of Wellington's victory at Waterloo by joining the Southeys for a large bonfire, and a rum punch-fuelled dinner, at the top of 'lofty Skiddaw': the fourth highest summit in England.

For the most part, though, I tried to remember the poetry itself. The blurring of the buildings of central London problematised Wordsworth's assertion — voiced in 'Musing Near Aquapendente' (composed in 1837 and first published five years later) — that the elevation to a high place facilitates a 'visual sovereignty' over the surrounding landscape. More than this, the disappointment of the embodied experience in suburban south-east London opened up thoughts of the younger Wordsworth who, in Book VI of *The Prelude*, recounts the pedestrian crossing of the two thousand metre-high Simplon Pass in southern Switzerland. Wordsworth recalls how, for his younger student self, the walk over the Alps promised to be an epiphanic moment; a 'spot of time' which would continue to feed the poetic imagination long after the fleetingness of the physical act. In actuality, however, Wordsworth — and his Cambridge friend,

Robert Jones — crossed the Alps in a state of unselfconsciousness. Wordsworth, in his poetic reconstruction of the (non-)event, recalls how he and Jones believed that they were still heading upwards to the highest point to be crossed; but, upon encountering a local peasant, they were dispiritingly informed that they had, in actual fact, already begun their descent: 'And all the answers which the man returned/ To our inquiries — in their sense and substance,/ Translated by the feelings which we had —/ Ended in this, that we had crossed the Alps.' Wordsworth's poetic achievement, however, is to transcend the matter-of-factness of this final line, and to circumnavigate the sense of loss generated by the underwhelming bodily experience, by celebrating the unfettered potential of the imagination: 'Our destiny, our nature, and our home,/ Is with infinitude, and only there —/ With hope it is, hope that can never die'. That is to say, Wordsworth, in looking back, cuts through the figurative clouds which descended as a result of this physical 'failure' and he attains imaginative clarity through an immersion in the 'invisible world' of interiority. The remembered experience of a high place, then, shapes the poet's imagination and, by extension, his autobiographical poetic utterances; but not in the ways in which he had anticipated when approaching the Sublimescape of the Simplon Pass on foot.

In spite of the contrasting topographical scales, thoughts on how Wordsworth imaginatively recasts spatial disappointment through the filter of memory came to mind as my Dad and I rested in this not-so-high place in south-east London. In addition, the failure to get a secure visual grip on the skyline of central London enabled me to imaginatively travel north and north-westwards to my own young son at home on the fringes of Morecambe Bay. I began to imagine a day when I might bring him to Telegraph Hill. Whilst my

Dad looked down towards Erlanger Road and back towards the late 1960s, I looked forward to a revisiting of the Hill.

As we slowly retraced our route to the Tube station, the soundtrack of birdsong and jet engines audible on Telegraph Hill was increasingly replaced by the quotidian hum of the buses, cars and taxis travelling along New Cross Road. As we were sucked back into the centre of the city, I started to think about one last textual reference in the form of Gaston Bachelard's conflation of phenomenology and psychoanalysis in *The Poetics of Space* (1958). In that influential book, Bachelard famously celebrates the verticality of the house and suggests that to climb the stairs to an attic room is to move towards and into an enclosed environment which provides perfect conditions for the complex entanglement of 'memory and imagination' that is 'the poetic daydream'. When walking back along the flattened topography of Euston Road, I started to reflect on how Bachelard's meditations on the experience of houses are perhaps equally applicable to the experience of walking up natural high places. I remember that a former colleague once derisorily dismissed Bachelard's prose as offering nothing more than 'vapid sonorities'. As I drifted through the streets of central London again, recalling earlier days spent in subterranean archives, I couldn't help but disagree. For me, Bachelard reveals much about the ways in which the experience of verticality — the high places — opens up the oneiric. The not-too-demanding walk up Telegraph Hill might not have facilitated 'visual sovereignty' over the cityscape; but the vertical movement on foot did create a space in which memory and imagination, retrospection and anticipation, could coalesce.

LAVENDER HILL

Liz Cookman

Dull grey skies. Commuters and casual shoppers buzz in and out of the station as I set off up the hill into an icy breeze. I'm climbing Lavender Hill: a hump of ancient glacial spew in the heart of Battersea, just north-east of Clapham Junction. The road, an eponymously named section of the A3036, is my guide through this wild urban landscape. It's a typically London thoroughfare, perennially thronging with grubby cars and lorries and bearded cyclists heading up to Westminster or down to Wandsworth, then on. At three quarters of a mile long and just under eighteen metres high — that's less than two tail-to-tail double-decker buses — Lavender Hill offers a tough climb, but I should be able to make it.

I follow the pavement, passing the first row of shops. School kids are beginning to swarm; a tumultuous army of blue blazers swagger into newsagents and fried chicken joints. A spit of rain falls in dark modicums on the floor. I walk against the flow of pedestrians and, a little way along the road's southern edge, come to Battersea Library — an old four-storey, red brick reference library with rosewood-coloured turrets that disappear into the murk above.

I'd been past here many times before and its gaudy posters and out-of-date notice boards are all familiar to me; so too are the rowdy pair drinking Kestrel Super Strength on the wooden bench near the entrance. Two men: one a ball of tattered tweed and matted blonde fuzz, the other wearing a huge winsome grin and a woolly hat so weathered it's more hole than hat. In the still moments, before the wind washes the air clean, their interesting perfume — of stale hangovers and festering bodily fluids — reaches my unwelcoming nose.

Despite being thoroughly sozzled, they shiver in the cold. It's been a mild winter, but the temperature has dropped and my hands and cheeks are beginning to feel it too — each terse lash of wind leaves my bare skin a little more raw. There will be a frost tonight; the gritty surfaces of shallow, greying puddles will freeze, but too many feet tread these pavements for it to last long. Ice rarely does in London. Once though, a long time before the city, this land was covered with ice.

During the last glacial period — the time when our current ice age was at its most extreme, around 18,000 years ago — harsh winters and freezing temperatures meant that vast sheets of ice formed that, at their peak, covered a third of the Earth's surface and claimed millions of gallons of water. Sea levels and rainfall plummeted. The air was starved of moisture and the land of colour

a barren monotony,

stillness

broken only by powdery

frost

drifting

across white plains. Much of Britain was like an Arctic tundra: a desert of wind and cold reaching all the way across Europe, unbroken by country borders or the North Sea which hadn't yet formed. Whole forests and mountain ranges were consumed by these 'rivers of ice': glaciers forced to move under the sheer weight of their own mass; solids that oozed and slid and behaved like liquid plastic. The ice slowly smothered everything, devastating the lands so that, when the world eventually began to warm and the glaciers retreated, our geography was changed forever. What hadn't been crushed or eroded by the ice was altered by epic floods with such force that new seas were formed, dividing us from mainland Europe and trapping the Thames which, until that point, had been a tributary of the ancient German river Rhine. The chewed up remains of the old land, carried in the bowels of the glaciers for thousands of years, became the raw material for a new terrain, for new hills and contours. Lavender Hill is one of these glacial dumps. Perhaps not the Ice Age's most mind-blowing achievement, but useful for anyone trying to get to Westminster from Wandsworth.

At roughly the same point as the library, and the bench where Scruffy Blonde and Smiley McGrubberson are bickering over a tab end, the earth deep below the modern city begins to change. Below the pavement and subterranean electricity cables, glacial gravel merges with Taplow gravel – the granular, sand-rich foundation of the Thames Terraces. The river is just over a mile away. It's these conditions – the good drainage and elevation – that helped give the hill its name: before the station brought an almighty wave of urbanisation just over one hundred and fifty years ago, this was agricultural land ribbed with colourful rows of sweet-smelling lavender. I try to imagine the aroma as I pass the two drunks and head onwards.

The road ahead is faced with a dense entanglement of shops and houses, it's noisy and cluttered: boxy council blocks and boarded-up boutiques; health food stores and posh estate agents.

Victorian terraced houses, mostly divvied up into newsagents and dim-windowed bedsits, watch over me as I climb the slope — the incline must be hitting a heady five degrees by now. The sky has turned pale and bright and I squint against the glare.

The pleasure in higher ground usually lies in perspective, the comfort one gets from feeling small against the vastness of the landscape. The chance to, as Robert Macfarlane puts it, 'look down on a city that I usually look across. The relief of relief... a way of defraying the city's claims on me.'[1] But Lavender Hill doesn't feel like a hill, despite the gradient. Most of the view is obscured by a thick fog of glass and brickwork; it hems me into the road. I can't see out and it dampens my senses. I've no concept of the topography of the outlying land or the direction of anything — there is only forward or back. I don't know if, beyond the buildings, the rest of the city is even there. For all I can see, this, right here, is everything.

The cheerful purple heads of lavender flowers yield abundant nectar meaning that, before the station brought an explosion of shops and houses that proved fatal to local farming, nearby bee hives were swimming in high-quality honey. As one of nature's perfect partnerships, together they brought farmers here a hearty revenue from the markets. Lavender was thought to protect against disease; a cure-all, it was burnt to cleanse sickness from the air and honey was used as a medicine. Sometimes the heavily-scented oil was used as a household cleaner or mixed with beeswax to make a fine polish. They were eaten together too, lavender added to honey to create an aromatic and indulgent treat.

---

[1]   Robert Macfarlane, *The Wild Places*, New York: Penguin, 2008.

At the approximate summit of Lavender Hill is Battersea Arts Centre. It was built in the late 19th century as the town hall of the now-defunct borough of Battersea, but is now a theatre and arts venue. I heave myself up the last hardy chunk of the ascent, then head inside for some well-earned refreshment. In the entrance hall I'm struck by an elaborate glass mosaic on the floor: a medley of blues, pale to bright, like a pool glistening under a hot sun, and all around, not much bigger than my foot and sort of floating, there are simple black and gold bee emblems. Some have their wings outspread as though poised for flight, others appear to be resting or feeding.

I sup a lukewarm latte in the ground floor café and ask around to see if anyone knows about the bees. Are they anything to do with local lavender? No one seems to be sure. A waitress tells me she overheard a walking guide say they were part of the original council's statement of intent: it would remind them to work hard and value teamwork. Another says she's sure they stand for BB, or Battersea Borough. Neither know anything about lavender.

Warm and slightly buzzing, I feel set to tackle the descent. So I hit the road again in the direction of Westminster, following the chewing gum-strewn pavement as it eases down the reverse of the hill. Ashen people wait at a bus stop under an ashen sky, shrinking into their scarfs and collars against the chill. In this light, there is little that doesn't appear grey: the houses with their peeling and water stained paintwork; the leafless bushes that spike up from behind low lying walls; the pitted tarmac and dirty pedestrian crossings and even a patch of grass, the front yard of the Ascension of Our Lord church, is also somehow sedate and drab.

Just near the next crossing however, a clearing catches my eye. It's a sudden and momentary break in the terraces and estates on the northern side of the road, a window out from this claustrophobic gloom. Two steps to the left or right and it would be missed, but from this one accidental spot I can see all the way across London. A view — at last.

I stop to survey the scene, soaking in the soothing magnitude of the distant landscape. I can see for miles across the tops of all sorts of buildings: the chimneys of Battersea Power station; the rolling crest of the London Eye then, tiny from here, the sharp apexes of Parliament and the BT Tower. It's an immense chain of manmade peaks, an architectural mountain range growing ever smaller as it disappears into the horizon.

People must have been admiring the view for thousands of years, yet it's unlikely any two viewings were ever alike. Once a glacial tundra, then farmland and now a huge network of glass and steel, bombastic monuments to money and power that are forever rising and falling, a scene that ebbs and flows from one season to the next just like any natural environment. Although the height of these structures greatly exceeds that of my tiny natural hill, it feels like I'm much higher than they are. I can see our position, Lavender Hill's place in the world, and be certain that I'm very, very small.

DENMARK HILL

Mary Paterson

I f you ever find yourself pushing a shoulder into the wind at the crest of Denmark Hill — perhaps you are steering a pram away from the roar of traffic, perhaps you are keeping to a gentle motion so as not to wake the baby — then your prize is to find the city laid out for you like a series of theatre flats. First: the utilitarian clutter of King's Hospital, a Lego-block sprawl that tumbles towards Camberwell. Next: the hopscotch path of Victorian churches, spires dotted from here to the horizon. And finally: the glamorous skyline of London's most recent landmarks — The Gherkin, The Shard, The London Eye — all shine and steel and lit up like Christmas trees, their sharp edges punching coloured lights into the clouds.

This is the surprise of south-east London: it offers a view back to the city. In an area networked by trains that don't run on Sundays and buses that crawl interminably up the Walworth Road, the panorama from Denmark Hill throbs with a reminder of what lies beyond reach. Colonised by the sprawling suburbs a century ago, the territory you are walking through now is a plantation of domestic architecture, fringed with a view. If you squint you can almost see a procession of sepia housewives pushing their prams up the hill, towards the smell of carbolic acid. They crane their necks to check how far they've come from the grime of the city. The miles are marked out in homely battlements: clean streets, clean windows, closed doors.

Perhaps you are listening for the soft, high whine of a

child that has started to stir. Perhaps you are watching for signs of movement beneath a pastel shroud. Perhaps you decide to take a turn through the dark wings of a thicket hedge onto the empty stage of Ruskin Park: thirty-six acres of lawn edged with tennis courts, a children's playground and a train line that ambles east to Peckham, west to Brixton, and beyond. Above you, an aeroplane tips its wings to start the circle of descent to Heathrow. Behind you, a row of suburban villas stares blankly at the magnificent view. At the bottom of the slope, a dry paddling pool waits open-mouthed for summer, and a woman much like you says in a voice much like yours, "Have you seen my baby?"

This modest summit stands between the mansions of Herne Hill and the tower blocks of Camberwell. Named as the hunting ground for Queen Anne's husband, Denmark Hill's woods have long been tamed by houses, and its grand mansions replaced by neat semis that sit shoulder to shoulder and too close together. The slums they used to look down upon have gone too: cleared initially for huddles of social housing and more recently for ladders of private apartments, their mean rooms concatenated into one another, prices rising every day.

At first you don't realise there is anything wrong. She speaks so normally, so casually. And you, perhaps, are watching the clouds for the first signs of sunset. You are waiting for dusk to close over the gates, the lawns, the fences, For Sale boards, Missing Teddy signs, lost mittens, deflated footballs, broken branches, the deserted portico, the empty bandstand and the steady motion of the long, suburban day. But then she says it again. "Have you seen my baby?" And you realise that her voice sounds like it has been caught on something sharp. She walks clumsily between pushchairs and children's rucksacks, addressing no one in particular. "He is two years-old. He is wearing a yellow scarf. He looks like me."

The suburbs were built for women and children: the manicured safety of parks and avenues, the discrete rations of private homes; all contrived to parcel up domestic life behind net curtains. Ruskin Park itself was assembled in 1907 on the ridge of the hill: a slice of recreation for the newly resident Edwardian lower middle class. It was named after the area's most prestigious tenant, John Ruskin — the great Victorian critic, artist and social reformer. He grew up half a mile away, educated in a drafty home by his mother, who did not believe in toys; and spent his midlife here, inches closer to the beat of the city.

Someone else has called the police. You scan the landscape for signs of an imposter. You are looking for anything that is too quick, too ungentle, too masculine. Fat-trunked oak trees raise their twisted fingers to the gods. A dog shivers in anticipation of a slow, fat squirrel.

"The house itself had every good in it," John Ruskin wrote of his home in Denmark Hill, "except nearness to a stream, that could with any reason be coveted by modest mortals." But unlike the squat villas that were built over his land, Ruskin turned his eyes away from London. He worked and slept in rooms that faced "straight south-east", his back to the view.[1]

Women have begun to congregate at the lowest part of the

---

[1]   John Ruskin, *Works*, "The Library Edition." eds. E. T. Cook and Alexander Wedderburn. 39 vols. London: George Allen, 1903-1912. Quoted in http://www.victorianweb.org/authors/ruskin/homes/13.html (accessed 11/12/13).

park, as if the shadow of the hospital will offer some protection. The hospital stares back, saying nothing. The women make a circle of bent backs, shielding each other from the railway line, the hum of the traffic and the splendour of the city.

The park stands in the grounds of eight demolished Georgian houses. All that remains of them now is one ruined portico — the orphaned frontage of 170 Denmark Hill, kept as a shelter by the park's planners. Perhaps it was meant to be a reminder of an earlier age, when buildings were grand and households were prestigious. Perhaps it was meant to be a totem for local ambition. Today the portico is boarded up with strips of plywood and surrounded by metal fencing: the kind used to control crowds at a public funeral.

Your instinct is to flee in the opposite direction — climb higher and higher, seek solace in perspective. But that would mean you were alone, and perhaps you don't feel comfortable being alone any more. Perhaps you have become accustomed to the dry-tongued small talk of nap times and feeding schedules. Perhaps you find it easier not to hold a thought for longer than the length of time it might take for a baby to drop a rattle. Together, you clasp prams and hoods and child-sized limbs until your knuckles go white. The children wriggle and try to escape.

When you first moved to this part of town, you took the lift up to the top floor of your building to see if you could look back to your old life, north of the river. In the moments before the baby started to whine, you thought you saw a hand waving from the top of the BT Tower. It was an illusion, of course — a smear on the glass that glistened when a passing cyclist waved his Day-Glo vest in your direction. You shepherded the pram downstairs and into the park. You counted eight hundred steps to pass the time. You walked towards the bandstand and paused to watch a trio of ducklings waddle from puddle to puddle. The ducklings started to approach. Motherless, they were looking for something to follow.

They say John Ruskin's claustrophobic childhood is what made the grown man so reserved. It's because he grew up in a joyless home, they say, with an over-protective woman, they say, that his marriage failed — annulled, scandalously, on the grounds of impotence. Despite his success, Ruskin never left the steady rhythms of suburban life. He brought his parents to live with him here, in Denmark Hill. Their rooms faced west, onto the walls of the front garden.

Last night you heard the sound of screaming. You opened the window and inhaled the smell of diesel. The sound, to your relief, was coming from foxes. But then you saw the men standing in the shadows, encouraging their dogs to rip the foxes to shreds. The animals yelled in terror, their eyes flashing round the car park of the Fox on the Hill, a triangle of tarmac with nowhere to hide.

Everyone is imagining what they would do if their child had vanished. Everyone is feeling their limbs go rigid with fear. You look up to see the glowing tip of Canary Wharf winking in the distance, pointing up, up, up to its achievements. You look down to see your helpless hands curled over the pram, rocking it in a gentle, steady motion. You wish that someone would reach out to the woman who is rocking beside you, making a noise like she is being drowned.

Your neighbours told you this was urban fox hunting. They told you it was executed by dogs that are bred to be vicious. The community support officer said there was nothing he could do.

The sky begins to darken. The surrounding villas start to glow. Outside the park, a cavalcade of police cars wails towards

London.

In public, John Ruskin was adored by women. When he lectured at Oxford University, they had to be banned from attending his talks because there was not enough room for the male undergraduates to sit down.

Train carriages rumble through the gloom, boxes of silhouettes with plugs in their ears and somewhere else to get to.

Perhaps, you think, it was Ruskin's ineptitude that made him so appealing. Perhaps he was an unthreatening man. Sheltered and benign, perhaps he spent his whole life in the clammy grasp of childhood.

She screams.

There is a yellow scarf trailing from the fence at the bottom of the slope.

A round face peers from the darkness. A childish face, soft and doe eyed, like his mother.

The boy had buried himself between the tennis courts and the railway track. The boy had folded himself inside the brambles with the lost balls, the missing toys, the single gloves, the beer cans, cigarette packets, broken glass, discarded wrappers and stinging nettles that run all the way from here to the end of the line.

You had to march three times round the bandstand before the ducklings left you alone. "I'm not what you're looking for," you muttered to the wind.

His mother sweeps him up and sobs into his hair. She carries him slowly, ungracefully, up the hill. He cranes his neck to look back at the crowded trains. Someone is ringing a bell to empty the park. The circle of backs splinters. Behind you, the city pulses into a network of mechanical heartbeats. Above you, branches dissolve into a navy sky. The baby kicks his blanket into the mud, and you push him on, keeping to a gentle motion, towards the south-east gate, towards home.

RICHMOND HILL

Martin Kratz

> There is a hill beside the silver Thames,
> Shady with birch and beech and odorous pine
> And brilliant underfoot with thousand gems
> Steeply the thickets to his floods decline.
> *Robert Seymour Bridges, 'There is a Hill'*

I am writing regarding the "expedition" you undertook to the slopes of Richmond Hill, Sunday 16th February 2014, to inform your piece for the anthology *Mount London*. I would like to object to the "facts" you established in the course of your '"research" there, and make some comments of my own, which I feel I am entitled to, as the subject of said piece.

If you are wondering at what point, I, a hill, became conscious of your intentions, then I was aware of your approach from the moment you drew level with Ham Common. You remember the Common of course, from your own failed childhood attempts at trying to kick a football there. You were driving a flashy rental car. You hired it in Manchester. You practically hummed with smugness about the upgrade. How could I not feel you coming?

I *feel* everything. Every footfall, wing beat and word around me. Everything. From the depth of the tread on the sole of your shoe, to the shape and motion of your pen across paper as it trembles down through your body. Think: a reverse-seismograph. I felt the sudden impulse that took you on route through Richmond Park instead of the road past your old school. I even felt your growing frustration, as the inevitable cavalcade of cyclists and Range Rovers on their Sunday outings prevented you from finding anywhere to park up top.

You eventually drove back down, out of the park and into Petersham village, in angry accelerative bursts, and were squeezed right to the bottom of River Lane, three car-lengths from the flood-swelled edges of the Thames. I should at least give you credit for the remaining local knowledge which found you that spot, and which left those vultures in their four-wheel-drive beasts, circling the erstwhile royal game park.

The moment you got out of the car, you started writing, using the roof for support. *A cormorant squats on a buoy, ring-necked parakeets chatter in the woods, the Thames is high around the ait, dogs lope across the meadow...* Your head was stooped over the paper as soon as you arrived. You hadn't even started walking yet. You know this scene by heart. This is home turf. You could have written that crap anywhere.

Right from the off, it was clear, that you had come already knowing what you were going to write: a sort of nature study on the flora and fauna of "Mount London"; a mosey up to Turner View in Richmond from where you would reflect on my various mountainous qualities. The story arc suggested itself: beginning/bottom — middle/top — end/bottom. Nice closed loop.

Not that your observations were entirely wrong. I can confirm for instance the results of your impromptu footwear survey: for the record, yes, nearly half the people rambling the Thames bank that day were wearing some kind of hiking boot. And yes, there is an "Alpine Restaurant" near the bridge selling *Bier und Bockwurst*. And yes, the Range Rovers and cyclists, have a certain mountain sports quality about them. Your point is not wrong, just forced.

You attempted to make of me a mountain, no matter how much I resisted. Yet at the same time, you were being so condescending towards the very mountainous features you needed to advance your case: the whole hiking-boot-Range-Rover-mock-Tour-de-Francing-*Bockwurst*-eating brigade. I bet you were overjoyed when your "expedition" was nearly cancelled due to extreme weather. Not because you wouldn't have to go—but because it just couldn't get more mountainous than that.

Let me ask you: was there anything you found here, that you did not already expect? I mean, a turn of thought that caught you off guard? That quickened or stopped you in your tracks?

If you run a giant finger down the Thames, after the scrape of the parade of trees, my slopes rise up suddenly and steeply to meet you. I have felt centuries of excavation and colonization, from the digging of prehistoric barrows to the mining of clay on my *land-slipped lower slopes*.[1] Looking across the river to Marble Hill and Strawberry Hill, the view extends all the way to Windsor, where the furry, dark line of the Great Park caterpillars across the horizon. This is from the Turner View: a pleasant composition consisting of Glover's Island (where *a cormorant squats*) drawing the gaze into an elegant river bend. Turner painted it, but in winter especially, it already looks like a Turner without being painted: the trees without their foliage appear brush-stroked.

Compared with the view on the other side into London, the

---

[1] Author's note: This oddly poetic line is from the Borough's information panel at the Terrace Gardens.

tree to building ratio looking outwards is overwhelmingly arboreal. The woods haze the view, proceeding in bands of lightening grey-scale outwards towards the horizon. Only a few steeples, blocks of flats, peek out in between. This is 'Richmond's self, from whose tall Front are ey'd / Vales, Spires, meandring Streams, and Windsor's tow'ry Pride.'[2]

The birdsong on the Terrace Gardens from where you looked, finally broke your concentration. You looked up and wandered like a stunned Roman augur, trying to take the auspices of the birds above the trees. But there were too many. Swan-diving pigeons, robins, gulls, thrushes, crows — the slow-motion descent airplanes on the Heathrow flight path — stopping and starting the view. The birds madly signaling, and you could only think in terms of coming disasters. Except, with the wide flood-pools on Petersham Meadows below, the swollen river, the broken-trunked tree toppled drunk over the railings, and the giant glass hull of The Ark building floating over Hammersmith, it appeared as if disaster had already struck.

To look the other way, into the city, you went to King Henry's Mound in the Park. This is my highest point, the supposed middle of your story. From here you would walk on, back to the car on River Lane, summarising me neatly, circling me off with your feet. Waving goodbye to the golden figure that rises above the cedars from All Saint's Church, which lifts its hands towards you in reply.

But if there is anything of me in this, then it must be that as a hill I will always encroach on your idea of what I am. Tell them, how when you looked through the telescope trained at St Paul's, it first

---

[2]   Alexander Pope, 'The Alley'.

seemed like you could reach out and grab the dome from ten miles away. A protected view over three hundred years-old. Yet the birds wouldn't let you be, and darted across your lens from Sidmouth Wood, still urgently communicating after the event. Constantly bursting in on your perfectly pre-composed image. And at the edges of the circle, cranes hung in over the dome, like youngsters photobombing a picture, the city continuously rising out of and over itself.

BRIXTON HILL

Karen McCarthy Woolf

[1] *On the left as you go up* Rush Common is the first place you arrive at. Set back from the road a tarmac path winds through it.

Thin green rag, remnant from the enclosures —

[2] *Some friends once lived in* a double-fronted Georgian on Brixton Water Lane. Their garden was large and L-shaped and a good proportion of it used to be the car park of the pub now called The Hootananny. Every year these friends held a party and I would go there and bounce on the trampoline with the children. The garden also had a well in it that sunk into the subterranean Effra.

Some other friends lived for a while in a flat on Josephine Avenue, where the back gardens are at the front, separated from the houses by pavement. Some of these gardens had locked gates and many others did not: mostly they were used by prostitutes and to park cars in.

[3] *At the apex* of the afternoon in summer, men carry folding Formica-topped tables down from the flats to play dominoes.

[4] *A windmill* is not what you expect to find, although there is also The Windmill on the street leading up to it where indie bands play. The pub has a low ceiling and the walls are covered in graffiti. There was once, also, a windmill on Morrish Road — the last or the first road in Brixton, depending on how you look at it.

[5] *The Nail Shop*:
  Nails £10
  Eyelash £10
  Shellak [sic] £20
  Threading £3
  Full set glitter £17
  Underarm waxing £5

[6] *At the House of Correction* 'A woman is a woman, and whatever her conduct or crimes may be her sex should be held sacred. The flogging of a negress is not one thousandth of a part so degrading and so afflicting as the labour of this torture wheel to an English woman.'

[7] *You set your limits, you decide* how much to spend, how long to play. Need help? Contact the national helpline on 0808 8020 133.

[8] *Amongst the pink hyacinths* outside Paradise Spice you will find chicken bones (stripped clean), many Dragon Stout and Guinness bottle-tops pressed into the earth, a £5 'Talk Home' phone card and an empty Smirnoff miniature. At the newsagents, on a small shelf near the door, there are magazines called *Black Men* and *Irish Tits* that turns out, on second glance, to be *Big Tits*, which then makes sense in a way that *Irish Tits* could not.

[9] *When the Olympics were on* I remember ascending the brow of the hill on a 59 as Usain Bolt won gold and a spasm of triumph surged from the barbershop as the crowd spilled out into the heat. Green, yellow and black flags were everywhere and the barber had erected a

gazebo over a soundsystem that thumped out an irresistible bassline into the twilight.

[10] *Things of elegant beauty* do not exist only in the past. That said, there is something bewitching about ladies with parasols in watercolours winding their way up grassy hillocks long since collapsed into Morley's and Rooster's Stop chicken shops.

[11] *A Jacobean chair* was the thing I had to have from the antique shop on the corner of Arodene Road. It was August, my dad was in the Royal Free and the air was dusty. I was on the phone when I bought the chair, distracted by the medical minutiae that surround the terminally ill. Buying the chair was something I could not afford to do, but the compulsion was overwhelming. The chair had diamond-shaped leaves carved on it and woodworm holes on the seat; the proprietor's father — a collector of 17th century furniture — assured me the worms were long dead, otherwise there would have been little piles of sawdust at its feet.

[12] *Things that are near yet far.* The top of the Hill when you are cycling up it in the bus lane. The bus as it pulls away from the stop after you've dashed across the road trying to catch it.

[13] *Even though I am not a Catholic* I went to Midnight Mass on Christmas Eve at the red brick church on the corner with a friend. On the way out we queued to receive a blessing from the new Father as the previous priest had died, suddenly, earlier in the year. I had to cross my arms over my chest to indicate I had not been baptized and was therefore forbidden to receive the sacrament.

[14] *Things that are far yet near.* Stanley Clare's Independent Funeral Directors with its plastic flower arrangements and marble scrollwork miniatures in the window that say things like 'Remembering you is easy Dad, it happens every day, missing you is something that never goes away.' Negril: in this case the Jamaican café on the hill, where a poet once wrote she was *slightly in love with the waiter.*

[15] *Things that make you feel nostalgic.* Here illuminated by the Tesco Metro colonizing the site of the old George IV — its parties were so late-night they took place in the day, hard house high-hatting out over the insomniac congregation. The protest occupation was futile and brief, coinciding, as it did, with new laws that made squatting a criminal offence.

[16] *Procedures when visiting* The Clink/Restaurant at Her Majesty's Prison — those looking to book a table will need to/all guests are asked not/mobile phones or SIM cards are not/cameras are not/ scissors, knives and sharp objects are not/chewing gum and aerosols are not/if your name does not/it is a criminal offence if you do not/

[17] *People who look as though things are difficult for them*: two little boys whose mother wears pink, pink and only bubblegum pink with a pink wig and a pink shopping trolley.

[18] *I remember* I came over from Guyana the day after the riots, my cousin lived on Bonham Road, that wasn't in '81 though that was '85, I forget which riot it was now, my friend had to walk up the hill because there was a bus they'd turned over, the worst thing though

was the fish and chip shop, everybody said why couldn't they leave off the fish and chip shop, that was community, it was their livelihood, the lady used to say, take that saveloy, pay me tomorrow, she was Greek, they were a family, they left soon after, they were disillusioned, their hearts weren't in it any more, that's what my aunt used to say, why couldn't the rioters leave them alone, why couldn't they be satisfied with Carpetland?

[19] *This prime position is/*a chic and/breathtaking/fantastic new/ beautifully presented/neutral/offering cool/delights of/vibrant/ wonderful/stunning/superb/unrivalled/exceptionally/sought after/enviably located/and secluded/private/secure gated/ vaulted/extending/chain.

[20] *When Laura was alive*
    she used to parade up and down
    in front of
        her kitchen window that looked out
        onto the prison yard, or stand on a chair
        to try to see over the outhouse
        with its slate roof that obscured
        the view, her long red hair
    cascading down her back.

[21] *Brixistan is the way* it used to be written and on p.493 of *The History of Antiquities of the County of Surrey* it says this village takes its name from a Saxon landowner 'Brixi' who demarcated the boundaries of his property with a stone.

[22] *It is important to document* Olive Morris House. You can take enquiries about benefits, council tax, housing and parking to this centre.

It is important to document Olive Morris. Black. Feminist. Panther. Squatter. Pictured with a megaphone, wearing a white vest, the arm that holds it up to her mouth is muscled. On the reverse of another, earlier photograph: 'taken at about 10pm on 15 Nov '69 after the police had beaten me up. King's College Hospital.'

It is important to document also that she said 'not a single problem associated with racialism, unemployment, police violence and homelessness can be settled by "rocking" against the fascists, the police or the army. The fight against racism and fascism is completely bound up in the fight to overthrow capitalism, the system that breeds both.'

If my father were still alive I would have rung him to find out if he knew her, because he was a community activist too, although not until just after the riots, and as Olive Morris was a feminist and he was never a feminist, and she died of cancer in 1979 when she was just 27, perhaps their paths may never have crossed; but she was Jamaican, and if he were alive, he would have told me, he would have insisted, how it was important to document that.

[23] *Yuck* is the word that was sprayed on the window of Foxtons when it opened on the High Street.

[24] *In a city time is expressed* through layers. Take for example the lamp-post from the original electrification in 1888, up high on the same stretch as The Telegraph, the pub where Basement Jaxx had a residency, now a Christian evangelist HQ that rents space

to a nursery and holds Zumba and yoga classes. This lamp-post resembles the lamp-post Jadis the white witch threw like a javelin in *The Magician's Nephew*. There is no lamp remaining, just a crossbar, around which a rope is wound that affixes two battered plastic palm fronds to the iron trunk. This refurbishment is all that remains of the Ghanaian restaurant, Iroko, whose owners decorated the whole strip like a beach promenade before it burnt to the ground barely six months later.

[25] *The border* is where the South Circular intersects the A23 — at the Wetherspoons the road widens to a dual carriageway and the crest of the hill plateaus before resuming its rise and eventual fall out to the coast.

[26] *On a bright moonlit night* as you pass the abortion clinic over the road from The White Horse, you can hear newly nocturnal wrens, songbirds that have changed their hours so they're no longer drowned out by the volume of traffic.

FOREST HILL

Edmund Hardy

F orest Hill is an idea, a generic name to sell a fresh start in the wooded hills of south London. It wasn't 'dreamed up' but rather very accurately described by a housing developer in the 1790s. Let's build an estate on a cloud and call it Cloud Town or Worldview Heights! It took me a long time to attempt an ascent of this suburban peak — go uphill from the station and you end up in Sydenham, a different place where they do things differently, or overshoot into Dulwich. A second and more mental approach was needed: to climb up inside a name.

The first marker came after I arrived and tried to cross the south circular as it kinks round in order to go under the railway. Fumes lay heavy in the cold so I hurried into British Red Cross to look at the books. On the threshold, I looked down and saw an ancient mosaic on the shop's step, child-like in its simplicity — amid curly foliage motifs it read, in a blue serif font, J. SAINSBURY. It looked like it was underwater, as mosaics often do to me — the individual tiles reflect light at different angles whereas my perception unifies these planes in order to make sense of the overall design or image. The angles distort the image and the effect is the assertively fragmented, shimmering quality of mosaic. Long since gone from this corner, mosaics, marble counters and white tiled walls differentiated Victorian era J. Sainsbury shops from competitor Home and Colonial who used to cover their floors in sawdust, or so I read on a board in the Sainsbury archives at the Museum of London Docklands where you can also see the first Sainsbury's loyalty card in a glass display case among other treasures.

From here, I took a circuitous route to take in art deco flats, a side alley where builders shouted down "Are you here for the studio?" (I wasn't), and a new house made of larch called The Larch House. I most enjoyed walking through a small estate of terraces built in ash-grey brick, particularly looking at one front garden of pampas grass, the white brushes waving in front of the silvery walls. This pleased me, although iridescent grey tones often do — I like the idea of a cinder estate, born from fire. Then amidst a sprawling estate from the seventies, I scanned for a possible peak. Houses step down the hill in terraces and little courts, and in the middle a larger paved area, an unused public space where the slabs are now uneven but the pathways lead around an octagonal segment from a church spire. It's the top of Christopher Wren's city church of St Antholin (of Budge Row), a church which was rebuilt after the great fire and then demolished in 1874 to make way for Victoria Street. Earlier, during renovations in 1829, part of the spire was replaced, and a Sydenham printer called Robert Harild bought the old segment for £5 and placed it in his garden. In the middle of the great farming of freehold land to grow interest for old families — landed estate dividing into villas and gardens, then terraces and infill — the spire has outridden these divisions, remaining in place as a Forest Hill folly. A cedar tree (perhaps also surviving from the older garden) breaks apart the paving slabs further and adds to the palimpsest of periods and purposes.

Engravings show the octagonal spire of St Antholin above the city, making the experience of walking round level with it giddy — am I flying, or has the church been buried? Neither, but you could shoot a close up scene against the sky for a London version of *Wings of Desire* — two angels in long coats sitting on the spire discussing the destiny of human love while watching the innocent folk of Catford catching buses, going to the library and growing old. Perhaps the Horniman Museum walrus could have a role. It's rare to see a Wren effect from the wrong perspective as usually his architecture fixes you in just the way he designed — his restless variations on the geometry of square and circle and how the two coincide or move into each other: St Stephen Walbrook combining a square floor plan and a vaulted dome into a space which seems to be a geometrical contradiction; or the cruciform plan of St Paul's which makes the great dome rotate within its colonnade as a pivot.

The octagon is the transition point — square becoming circle or vice versa — and Wren buildings use the octagon sparingly, perhaps because it stabilises the transition between square and circle rather than creating it, and because its long history in sacred building types left little room for variation. But to treat his buildings as a genre, we could consider Wren's octagons at three levels — interior, plan and icon: the octagon room at the Greenwich Observatory; his eight-way street patterns for a planned rebuilding of the city post-fire; and his octagonal spires. St Bride's stellated spire is an octagon with another octagon shooting out, and then another and another, whereas the octagonal peak of Forest Hill is simpler, ribbed at each corner and tapering. It looks like a font, traditionally (that is, before the Reformation) octagonal in shape, following the earlier baptistery buildings which were often also based around eight — the octagon, in transition from a square plot of earth towards the circle of heaven, although no south London district can fairly be read as a giant font, washing the city clean of its sins. Shadowy portals gape at the bottom of each side, originally looking like a crown or lantern from the street but now giving this apparent font — face to face — a monstrous, hungry aspect. To be baptised and digested by a Wren in the same stroke, the fastest route through the world from innocence to salvation via architecture.

It was mid-morning and the time for fantasy was over; time to descend to the ornate glass house of Forest Hill's most famous collection of stuff paid for by thirst, Horniman the tea merchant's museum where I could warm up and consider routes down into Peckham. Scanning the museum for possible building forms, I found a long case clock with glass windows into rooms filled with dolls house people and furniture — a tick-tocking skyscraper or time tower.

From the gardens I looked across the valley to the edge of the suburb, a wall dividing it from Dulwich — a pair of high, inscrutably shaped forms, a brick ridge of three hundred flats: Dawson's Heights, Southwark council housing built between 1964 and 1972, designed by Kate Macintosh. After the reveries of Wren in the railway suburb this is a mountain which takes us into the twentieth century. It's a design deliberately caught in a transition, a statement born from different, simultaneous purposes. One example: the balconies could only be justified (under a Labour government accused of overspending) by having multiple functions, e.g. fire escapes but with 'break glass to enter' doors effectively creating private balconies for each flat but not under that name on the plans.

The transition is between an architecture which would reorder society and one which would try to mirror or serve it (this dialectic was within public architecture at this point but it would become associated with public vs private development) and it is captured everywhere in this design: monolithic but in brick and not concrete; twelve storey slab blocks descending at their ends in ziggurat steps to two storeys; following the contours of the hill yet extending and transforming it; dramatic in mass and grouping but self-negating in its trailing away into lines and shadows. If this is an arrangement of blocks, then each flat must cross between divisions and axes, the outside suggests. This irregularity of form gives all three hundred flats a balcony and two-thirds a view both north and south. The great, open puzzle of this interlocking, multi-functional irregularity completely side-steps the 'castle' or defensive trope which appealed to so many council estate architects of the period.

The buildings look like stacks of containers — in short like a megastructure, although none of the flats could be removed or rearranged, plugged in or out, as the core-and-module principle of most mega-ideas in the mega-craze of the '60s dictated. If it's a megastructure then that term would have to be stretched into the construction of a hill — a second, ordered rock formation upon the earth. Beneath Dawson's Heights, the contours of the hill itself are stabilised and constructed, down into the ground, not only by deep foundations but by great buttress drains which dry out the London clay to stop it sliding down to flatten Dulwich on one side and Forest Hill on the other, rendering the latter just a name beneath the clay once more. The drains, ten metres apart and six metres deep (the civil engineer James Dallaway wrote about the project in the Dulwich Society Newsletter), are full of easily draining granular material, an earthwork inserting veins of loose rock into the clay. I climbed this double construct — up some public stairs and onto a walkway, and the view straight across London to the northern heights, Canary

Wharf and the Dome was, finally, the social, open summit of Forest Hill. It's a polemical perspective, the yellow towers of Southwark and Lewisham's estates appearing as piles, shoring up the financial glimmer above them.

GIPSY HILL

Amber Massie-Blomfield

I t is not a good day to be outside. My umbrella has already blown inside out. My shoes are giving off an aroma like a dog that's been out in the rain.

I'm here to climb Gipsy Hill. At the bottom is a soggy patch of greenery running alongside Dulwich Wood Avenue, too unlovely to have a name, and today, too muddy to be walked on. Leafless trees stretch thin limbs from waterlogged roots to the sky. Things are getting tumbled: bins, estate agent signs. Empty plastic bags scuttle up and down the pavement and in little wind-whipped circles. The hill stretches up ahead, a grey strip of road ascending between two neat rows of houses towards a grey sky, clouds heavy with rain.

The weather has been like this for weeks. The news is all pictures of waves breaking over seawalls, famous landmarks half submerged, grandmas being piggybacked by strapping chaps in galoshes.

Ragnarok is a few days' away: the official date of Armageddon according to Vikings, when the sun will be devoured by a giant wolf. On my Facebook feed there are photos of jolly looking bearded fellows having parties in York. People are joking about this being the end of the world. It's all in good humour. But when I really think about it, what the end of the world might be like, I imagine it would begin a bit like this.

There were travellers here once, as the name suggests. Throughout the 18th and 19th centuries, the Romany population based in Norwood grew to be the biggest in London. They became celebrities, attracting the great and the good out of the city in their droves to experience, first hand, the power of gypsy magic. Samuel Pepys wrote in his diary in 1688 of his wife going with her friends to see 'the gypsies of Lambeth to have their fortunes told'. In 1777, they inspired a pantomime, *The Norwood Gypsies*, performed at the Theatre Royal, Drury Lane.

The Queen of Gypsies was Margaret Finch, who lived beneath an ancient oak in Norwood Park. An etching from the time shows her crouched in a mossy hollow, smoking a long pipe, two small dogs and a mug of something robust-looking at her feet. Her brow is furrowed but her lips are touched with a slight, mysterious smile.

None of these buildings would have been here. Until the arrival of the Crystal Palace in 1854 and Gipsy Hill railway station soon after, this was woodland, a rural stopping off point between London and Croydon. Its virtue would have been its height, the vantage point it offered on the comings and goings from the city, the temperamental shifts in the weather. London was a faint smoky patch in the distance.

Gipsy Hill.
Roman Rise.
Beggars Hill.
Rommany Road.

I say them to myself as I begin to climb.

I've been told my granddad came from a Romany family. They were gypsy horse traders from Edmonton in north London. I have dark hair and dark eyes, inherited from him. I ask my aunt about this history and although she doesn't know much about it, she says she thinks she has gypsy blood because she has always had the feeling of wanting to roam, she's just never had the chance.

My granddad likes to roam too. Now well into his eighties, he spends less than half the year in the UK: the rest of the time he is overseas, managing his various business enterprises or visiting colourful new countries.

He was born in Australia in a hut with no floor and my aunt tells me he and his brother used to ride to school on horses that would wait for them outside and take them home again. They came back to the UK, and when he was fifteen he ran away and joined the Fleet Air Arm. He's never talked to me about his Romany background, and I've never felt able to ask. I think of my family as practical people, not much given to the mystical connection with nature that I imagine good gypsy stock should have. But when I think about it harder I remember: my Grandma charming warts off other family members. It worked, every time.

My uncle is a barefoot walker; on Clare Balding's *Ramblings* he shared with the listeners of Radio 4 how this pastime helped him to deal with mental health issues. It is a firmly held belief in our family that a headache or a back pain can be cured by 'earthing': walking with bare feet in the grass.

It is one of the things I miss about living in the city: how rarely I get the chance to walk in bare feet on the grass.

Just off Gipsy Hill there is a 1960s block of council flats: Pear Tree

House. It is built into the side of the hill, an expanse of dull brickwork and glass with eight two bedroom flats and then, where the ground falls away, a windowless floor with a large, slightly rusty metal door.

You would never guess to look at it that this was once 'South East London's War HQ'. I suppose this is the point. Behind the door, and extending beneath the lawns and patios that stretch away down the hill, there is an eighteen room nuclear bunker, at one time housing an 'Intake Room,' a 'Control Room', a 'Scientific Advisors Room', a 'Health and Welfare Room', and all the other rooms one might need in the event of a nuclear disaster. It isn't possible for me to get inside. But I find photos of banks of colourful 'alert state' lighting and walls plastered with vast sprawling maps of the city.

It was built in 1963, in the wake of the Cuban Missile Crisis, a time when the fearful magic of the split atom was ripe in the public imagination. Then, in the 1980s, Lambeth Council announced that the borough was a 'nuclear free' zone and evicted the Civil Defence Authority, shutting down the building. Their logic presumably being that this declaration precluded them from any risk of being on the receiving end of a nuclear attack.

Nuclear armaments I suppose must still be a threat. At the time of the missile crisis only four countries were in possession of nuclear armaments, now The Federation of American Scientists estimates that there are nine. Our fears, however, have moved on.

In 1963 my granddad was twenty-seven years-old, living in Lossiemouth, a military base in a remote corner of Scotland by the sea. He shared a caravan with my gran and my eight-year-old mum.

My mum talks about the sense of camaraderie between the families that lived there. Because it was so remote, she says, there was a terrific sense of freedom. She remembers playing hide and seek in the banks of long grass that surrounded the base, where every so often, they would spot a wild cat. My granddad set up a club in an old Nissen hut, threw fancy dress parties and held poker matches. He ran an old field telephone from my mum's bedroom across the site to the back of the bar. If she ever wanted to get hold of them in the night, she had to crank up the handle and a sound like an aircraft siren would go off in the club.

1963 was the year of 'The Big Freeze'. It began snowing on Boxing Day and there was still snow on the ground that Spring. For six weeks no one could come or go. My grandparents didn't work. They walked my mum to school every day and picked her up at the end. The banks of snow built up around the road like a tunnel. It didn't melt until the end of May.

Half way up Gipsy Hill I stop at a trendy looking 'beer pop-up'. This is a fairly average suburban London street: a mish-mash of Victorian terraces and semis, including one in a pleasing taramasalata hue, and a few more recent blocks of flats that have sprung up in the gaps. Corner newsagents and the fish and chip shops you could find on any high street.

But the presence of this pop-up, along with the gastro-pubs and expensive 'vintage' shops at the top of the hill in Crystal Palace, signifies the recent arrival in the area of a set of arty young urbanites, priced out of the hipster strongholds of Stoke Newington and Dalston, or having outgrown them, seeking areas with better parks, better air, better views. I am amongst their number.

I order myself a pint and take a seat on a thin wooden bench along the wall. It is a small room, and although there are only a couple of people when I arrive, it soon fills up. People come in shaking veils of rain off their umbrellas, discarding waxed jackets to reveal patterned jumpers underneath.

At the table next to me, a couple on an awkward first date is talking in too-loud voices. They take in safe territory: the friends they have in common, cycling, what they think of the snacks. He is a real ale aficionado, and offers some reflections on the merits of each of their pints, which he sips, noisily, some of the froth getting caught in his moustache.

Talk turns to the weather. He has views on Nigel Farage, the political implications of what kind of shoes you wear for a flood. This is how the English will deal with the end of the world, she says. We will be worrying about the footwear.

My grandfather has been working on a system that can harness the power of the sea. The system uses long hydraulic cylinders moved up and down by the waves, which capture power as the internal pistons pressurise the oil. This pressure is passed to a motor to rotate the generator at an acceptable speed to suit the electrical frequency. He has won awards. He was invited to visit NASA.

This could change things, he says. It could have a part to play in reversing the damage we're doing to the environment, before it is too late. I say I think it is already too late, we're way beyond the tipping point, we're screwed. He is disappointed in me. What I'm lacking, he says, is faith.

Christ Church is situated towards the top of the hill. There has been a church on this site since 1862, arriving soon after the Crystal Palace to serve the influx of new residents: first a temporary iron building, and then, in 1867, a fine, Grade II listed ragstone edifice.

It was destroyed by a fire in 1987, the cause of which never appears to have been established. Only the tower remained, and when it was rebuilt it was turned into a private residence. A new building was constructed on the site of the old church; all clean lines and reflections. A large black cross is stark against the cream stone.

It is an Anglican parish church, I learn from the website, dedicated to serving the local community in and around Gipsy Hill. Wide in variety — different ages, cultures and personalities — all share a desire to follow Christ together and apply their faith in the real world.

I peer through the window. It looks calm inside, and dry. I try the doors. They are tightly shut and bolted.

At the top I stop and look back. Gipsy Hill is one of the highest points in London, and the view is one of the things that has drawn me back here over the years. You can see a long way. I'm not the only one admiring it. In fact everyone that passes seems compelled to stop and look out for a few moments, in spite of the lousy weather.

The glossy ribbon of road falls away into an expanse of scrubby greenery, the red points of Dulwich College, and beyond it, the domed roof of St Paul's, the audacious skyscrapers of the City and most prominently The Shard, the tallest building in Western Europe, which strains towards the sky away from the city like a spire. Right now, there's a smudgy half rainbow cutting through the clouds towards it. The city fades away on to the horizon.

I imagine Margaret Finch standing next to me. I think about

how the view has changed, and wonder if she would be impressed by it.

But I don't think she would have been much impressed with anything. Legend has it that when she died in 1740 (aged one hundred and nine) she was buried in a large square box seated upright. She was so accustomed to sitting with her knees tucked up under her chin that her sinews had contracted and she was unable to move out of this position. This doesn't suggest a person given to extravagant displays of emotion.

Life began to change for the Norwood Gypsies at the end of the 18th century. The Society for the Suppression of Vice brought charges, and a number of them were arrested under the Vagrancy Act. By the mid 19th century, the gypsies finally deserted Norwood. Soon after the Crystal Palace arrived in the area bearing new wonders: the world's first aeronautical show. Thirty-three life-size model dinosaurs.

We went to visit Lossiemouth a few years ago. When we got there, everything my granddad remembered — the rows of caravans, the picket fences, the concrete paths, the corrugated tin building that housed the club, the street lamps and the wires strung between them — all of it had disappeared, and what was left was just an expanse of grass, casually grazed upon by a few rugged looking sheep. The only trace of what had been there was a traditional red telephone box right in the middle of the field, now choked with a thick bramble bush, heavy with berries.

I asked him if he felt sad that so few signs of his life here remained.

He shook his head.

That's what happens, isn't it, he said.

When man goes.

Nature takes over again.

I decide to try a spell myself. I'd like to have a go wind whispering. This is the first magic a gypsy learns. You lie on your back beneath a tree with a question in mind. You close your eyes and listen to the wind moving through the leaves. If you are attentive, you will hear the answer to your question.

But the ground is muddy and the regimented line of bare London Planes outside the council block don't look like they'd be given to divulging juicy secrets.

Instead I think I'll try to do something about this weather. I find a spell: concocted for laundry days when the elements are unobliging, but applicable in a variety of situations. The knack is to inhale all the wind, and then blow it back on itself, in the direction that it came.

Gipsy Hill.
Roman Rise.
Beggars Hill.
Rommany Road.

I take a deep breath in.

CRYSTAL PALACE

Three Walks to Find the Highest Point

Gemma Seltzer

Walk One: Sydenham Hill Giant (1614)

O nly the single red bulbs marking the edges of the transmitter tower break darkness. This is Norwood Ridge, I say, as we walk, finding small pleasures in the long vowels. Once, it was part of the Great North Wood, which extended all across London. We are in the day's first dusty light, when the park is largely in shadow. I can barely see my own feet. Your hazy outline says that Hansel and Gretel were probably abandoned here, desperate, never to find their way home. I think it reassures you to map your experience onto a story you already know, rather than accept that you and I, in our waterproof coats, with our flasks, with our hand-drawn maps, are exploring the summit of Crystal Palace Park in the early hours; we have no equipment or technical knowledge and our boots are already gathering damp around the heels.

We are here because of the Sydenham Hill giant. An oversized man who merrily, ferally, lived amongst the trees in underground hollows a couple of centuries ago. He knew the exact point where the hill was its highest, where the hollyhock plants grew. One hundred and twelve metres, my notes tell me. I want to slowly pace this same half-mile stretch at the top of the park until we find the absolute peak. I think walking connects us to the earth, so the more we walk, the more sensitive we become to the rhythms of the ground. Therefore, we will naturally find the precise place. You, promised croissants and coffee for joining me, reluctantly agree.

It is a warm morning. As we pause to stare at the inky six o'clock sky, I reflect that I am more myself on ancient woodland. On hectares that were once oaks, hornbeams, bluebells and wild garlic, I tread as me. Standing in a high place that was hill before it was not, I feel my limbs loosen. We follow a pathway that was once the front wall of the old Crystal Palace. You jog ahead and throw your arms around one of the stone sphinxes. Tell me a riddle, you say. The sphinx says, no.

The story goes that a local child fell in a fire. Rather than ask the giant directly for the hollyhock spot, the villagers set a vast trap into which he stumbled, but escaped, except for a single finger. As we stroll, I say, losing a finger is not like losing other things like a tooth, coins or a sock. Those can be replaced. Without a finger, you can't point the way, can't scratch an itch. You can't express the number five with one hand.

We're at the end of the path. Closed, says the water-faded sign on Crystal Palace Museum. Its driveway is empty except a wooden barrel and the inner pages of a magazine flapping with five versions of the same sad face. The headline reads The Day We Nearly Won the Lottery. Moist leaves of cedar trees shine in the rising light. We walk the route back, watching as the view over south London and Kent reveals itself. Before the city grew upwards and outwards, it might have been possible to see other views too: a tiny woman pegging white squares onto a line in Southwark, a miniature baby opening and closing its fists at a gull by Tower Bridge, and small ships rolling along the River Thames. We turn to complete the route again.

An hour or so later, you finally stop and scuff your foot on the ground. People are with dogs, wearing flat caps and padded jackets. Two sirens belt out in quick succession. What happened to the giant, again? you ask. He uprooted the entire hollyhock batch for his bleeding hand, so the highest point was lost. Regretful, the people from the village placed the abandoned finger where the plants once grew. You crouch down and gather a pile of stones. Eighteen times we've walked this same path, and I'd not believed one specific area to be the crown. Standing on your modest mountain, arms folded, you say, I reckon it's here.

Walk Two: Brunel and His Sister (1854)

We look for a peak from another era. It's chillier for our walk this time: we wear thermal underwear. I have ropes, some experience in fancy knot-tying and ambition. You and I enter at the south entrance, by the boating lake and the prehistoric animals looming from between willow trees. We pass the concrete beauty of the National Sports Centre, then the concert bowl and its echoing acoustics, which makes walking by a strange, rumbling experience. Finally, we make our ascent.

Isambard Kingdom Brunel has an older sister called Mindy who is afraid of low places. The family lives on the fifth floor of a town house, extend all their furniture with stilts and place their daughter's bed on a platform. The two children climb fences, build castles from blocks, roar like mountain goats on rocky slopes. As adults, Mindy nurses soldiers in a hospital in the French Alps. Brunel studies engineering and the Old Testament.

The high point we chose to uncover next on Sydenham Hill is not the glassy, classy conservatory that houses the Exhibition of the Industry of all Nations, otherwise known as the Crystal Palace, but Brunel's two tall towers, built to feed elaborate fountains with jets of water that reach hundreds of feet high. Or, depending on whether you believe in historical accuracy, built to view a sibling across the English Channel.

Brunel is asked to amend the proposed design for the towers, ensuring the water tanks can be slotted in the upper section. At first he declines, reluctant to manage another engineer's work. Then, he considers that the Palace is a peak upon a peak and that the towers would be two peaks upon another peak. For a lover of heights, the doubleness appealed. The towers he constructs climb higher than the Palace, which at forty-one metres high on that one hundred and twelve metre hill, are seen across the city. The north and south towers are eighty-six metres tall on a one hundred and twelve metre hill that lead to cascades and landscaped gardens. The total of eighty-six metres is significant for Brunel, being both the number of miles (multiplied by ten) between his home and Mindy's and that of the many languages created by the destruction of the Tower of Babel.

You and I, that day, visit the base of the north tower but find metal railings prevent us from close investigation. This tower once had a cafeteria in its base, and was attached to one of the largest aquariums of the era. Disappointing, you say. Deep excavations, I reply, reading the notices. By the south tower, adjacent to the museum, we can lick bricks and touch the exposed piping. Gazing up, we imagine the mountainous structure, now a ghost in the landscape. Where was the exact centre of it? I tie a rope around my waist. You peer into the gated archway, and rub a finger on the rusting iron. It carried upwards smoke from the furnaces under the Palace, I say, without understanding how. With the end of the rope tied to a loop on the wall, I start to run until I'm jolted to a stop. You take a tree branch and mark the point I reached on the gravel. Here, you say.

Walk three: Veronica Maxim without wings (1904)

In the summer of 1901, a scientist called Gerald Levander steps onto a patch of warm grass and, wiping sweat from forehead, shading hands to eyes, forms a new theory. He writes a pamphlet called 'The Way Forward is Upward' (Chicago Press) stating that the earth is rising. The number of hills is increasing, he writes, and this is because the core is expanding, lifting the land. His calculations state that in four years the sky will be only half the distance away. I have already studied the essay and, though unlikely, begin to believe it is true.

This is our third walk and you make clear you that you accompany me only for the meals I offer as reward. You and I stand on a patch of grass not far from Crystal Palace station and consider this point. Levander's philosophy spreads from the US to the UK, taking New York, a bit of France and a few people in Belgium, before it lands in the hands of Londoners.

Meanwhile, Veronica Haynes is born, grown and frustrated in Boston. Veronica meets Hiram Maxim, an engineer, an inventor and a tease, at a masked ball. From the piano on which she is dancing, she topples into his arms. He fusses a little with divorce and compensation to his family, and then, in 1881, joins the London offices of the US Lighting Company and moves to the village of

West Norwood. In the month it takes to pack and say farewell to friends, Veronica also practises her English accent. She can manage "tomarto" as well as "hallo" and "indurstrial revorlution."

Their house has two barns and they hold weekly parties with dancing girls and fireworks in one. In the other, Maxim lays down his tools and notebooks. Learning of Levander's work one day he is alarmed by a powerful thought. If the sky is getting closer, then it will be easier to see. In his workshop, he starts to attach wings and engines to inanimate objects. He stands on Sydenham Hill, with an umbrella and pokes upwards. With a large stick, he pokes. He ties together a paddle and a shotgun and a slim rotting tree trunk, and pokes. How to touch clouds? How can many people, in the same moment, touch clouds? How could the experience of touching clouds mirror the sensation of touching the dreamy, fluffy things?

Maxim builds a new machine and makes it happen. Ten gloriously bright limbs extend from a central post, all linked by a spider's web of wires from which individual pods hang. Veronica spills her sweet wine and calls them ghastly flying machines. Single passengers grip the edge of their capsule and give in to the spin, finding themselves high above the ground, swinging up, reaching out for the sky.

Sir Hiram Maxim's Captive Flying Machine ride is installed in Earl's Court in 1904. This is followed by an updated version fixed on Hampstead Heath. Here, flying pods, a few metres long, carry up to twenty passengers. Bat and ball sets are provided for revellers to play within each pod, which proves incredibly popular.

Veronica Maxim is the first person to try the machine later established in Crystal Palace Park, replacing the old rotunda. I look at a series of old maps to estimate its location, because seeing where

I am and where I'll never be — the past and the present existing together in the same frame — is my kind of exciting. I imagine how Mrs Maxim climbs aboard, a capsule to herself, and waves to the crowds below. She raises her champagne flute. Her lipsticked mouth smiles and her face says, this is what happens when you marry a man who spends his nights hammering and measuring and scratching his chin. A brave soul is she: there are no seatbelts.

Full speed is slow by today's standards. Imagine a grown man sneezing, without a tissue to hand, and the speed of his nose juice across the room. It was much slower than that. Still, when a person jumps out of a moving capsule, it does take a few moments before they hit the ground.

This must be the third highest peak, after the Palace and the towers, I decide. We spend an afternoon circling an open space that was once home to fairground rides and air balloon launch points. Now, there is only thistles and patches of mud, overgrown grass on uneven earth. Somewhere here is higher than somewhere else. I feel lighter with the idea of this flying machine, as though my body is no longer solid and made of flesh and hair and many types of bones. Grasping my left wrist and then my right, ignoring my yelps, you ask me if I want to fly. You spin me around and around, and around some more. When you finally let go, I keep on turning, stumbling, and moving towards the fluid horizon until I eventually trip over my own heels and land crooked on the grass.

That's your spot, you say.

AUTHORS' NOTES

MATT D. BROWN has edited *Londonist.com* for almost a decade. He's obsessed with London and enjoys nothing more than poking around in sewers, warehouses, archives, catacombs and steeples. His writing has appeared in the *Guardian*, *Telegraph*, *Time Out*, *Nature* and many other places. He's currently working on his first solo book, which will, of course, be all about London.

SARAH BUTLER writes novels and short fiction, and has a particular interest in the relationship between writing and place. She has been writer-in-residence on the Central Line and at Great Ormond Street Hospital. Her debut novel, *Ten Things I've Learnt About Love*, is published by Picador in the UK and in fifteen languages around the world.

TOM CHIVERS was born in Herne Hill, south London in 1983. His publications include *How to Build a City* (Salt, 2009), *The Terrors* (Nine Arches, 2009), *Flood Drain* (Annexe, 2014) and, as editor, the anthologies *City State: New London Poetry* and *Adventures in Form* (Penned in the Margins, 2009 & 2012). He has made site-specific, perambulatory and audio work for Southbank Centre, Bishopsgate Institute, the Eden Project and LIFT. An award-winning independent arts producer, he is former co-Director of London Word Festival and currently runs Penned in the Margins from a small office in Aldgate. He lives in Rotherhithe.

LIZ COOKMAN is a writer and landscape enthusiast from London. She's mostly interested in being creative with real life stuff (non-fiction) and her work often focuses on nature, decay and urbanity. She has an MA in Nature and Travel Writing and has written for and edited various publications.

DAVID COOPER was born in Liverpool. He lectures in English literature at Manchester Metropolitan University where his research focuses on the literature of landscape, space and place. His recent academic publications include the co-edited collection of essays, *Poetry & Geography: Space & Place in Post-war Poetry* (Liverpool University Press, 2013), and he is a founding co-editor of the online scholarly journal *Literary Geographies*. He lives in Lancaster.

Tim Cresswell is a geographer-poet who has published widely in poetry magazines in the UK. Since moving from London to Boston in the summer of 2013 his work has started to appear in American and Canadian magazines including *Riddlefence*, *Spiral Orb* and *Soul.Lit*. His first collection, *Soil*, was published by Penned in the Margins in 2013. He is currently working on his second collection, *erratic*. He is also the author of five books on the themes of place and mobility.

Alan Cunningham is a writer from the north-east of Ireland. His first book, *Count from Zero to One Hundred*, was published by Penned in the Margins in 2013. He has published shorter work with *3:AM Magazine* and *gorse*. Based in London, he is currently working on a text interwoven with copious quotations from *The Green Fool* by Patrick Kavanagh.

Joe Dunthorne grew up in Swansea and now lives in London. His debut novel, *Submarine*, was adapted for film by Richard Ayoade and his second, *Wild Abandon*, won the Encore Award. A pamphlet of his poems was published by Faber and Faber.

Inua Ellams was born in Nigeria in 1984 and is an internationally touring poet, playwright and performer. He has published two poetry pamphlets: *Candy Coated Unicorns and Converse All Stars* and *Thirteen Fairy Negro Tales*. His first play *The 14th Tale* (a one-man show which he performed) was awarded a Fringe First at the Edinburgh Festival Fringe and his third, *Black T-Shirt Collection* ran at the National Theatre. He is currently working on a new play, *Barber Shop Chronicles*, a poetry pamphlet, *#Afterhours*, and his first full collection, *Of All The Boys of Plateau Private School*.

KATY EVANS-BUSH'S poetry publications are *Me and the Dead* and *Egg Printing Explained* (Salt), and *Oscar & Henry* (Rack Press). She writes the blog *Baroque in Hackney*, and lives in London.

SJ FOWLER is a poet, artist, martial artist and vanguardist. He works in the modernist and avant garde traditions, across poetry, fiction, sonic art, visual art, installation and performance. He has published five books, including *Enemies: Selected Collaborations* (Penned in the Margins, 2013) and been commissioned by the Tate, Mercy, Liverpool Biennial and London Sinfonietta. He is the poetry editor of *3:am Magazine* and is the curator of the Enemies project.

BRADLEY L. GARRETT is a writer, researcher and photographer based in the School of Geography and the Environment at the University of Oxford. Brad has a particular interest in uncovering hidden places in soil, seas, cities and space and has worked as a terrestrial and maritime archaeologist throughout the Aughts. His first book, *Explore Everything: Place-Hacking the City* (Verso Books 2013), is an ethnographic account with urban explorers, photographers of off-limits urban environments.

EDMUND HARDY is a London-based editor, writer and curator. His archive poem based on British army court martial transcripts, *Desertion*, was published by Arthur Shilling Press, and a critical book on dialectic, poetry and history, *Complex Crosses*, is forthcoming from Contraband Press. With James Wilkes he edits a press dedicated to the literary essay, Capsule Editions. At Parasol Unit, Islington, he curates a quarterly live event series connected to each exhibition.

JUSTIN HOPPER is a writer from Pittsburgh currently living and working in London. His recent work explores themes of landscape, memory and myth through audio poetry pieces (the *Public Record* and *Ley Line* series). He is currently working on a book, *The Old, Weird Albion*, about alternative visions of Englishness along the South Downs Way.

Martin Kratz is an associate lecturer in English at Manchester Metropolitan University. His poetry has been widely published in magazines including *The Rialto*, *Magma*, *The Interpreter's House* and *The Moth*. As a librettist, he collaborates regularly with the composer Leo Geyer, and their projects include the prizewinning song cycle *Sideshows*. Their chamber opera *The Mermaid of Zennor* was described by *The Times* as 'imaginative and beautifully shaped.'

Amber Massie-Blomfield began writing for theatre, and as a playwright has had work produced at Theatre Royal Bath, Tricycle, ICA, Tobacco Factory, Camden People's Theatre and internationally. As a short story writer she has had work selected by Are You Sitting Comfortably?, Story Tails, Antlers Press and The Ghastling. She is an Associate Artist with Annexe Magazine, who published her short story pamphlet *The Audience Member*. She has performed stories at festivals including Leefest, Beaconsfest and Interrobang?! By day she is Head of Communications for the Albany, Deptford.

Karen McCarthy Woolf was born in London to English and Jamaican parents. She is a PhD candidate at Royal Holloway where she is exploring the relationship between ecological poetry, elegy and hybrid forms. She has taught creative writing widely, notably for the Southbank Centre, Photographers' Gallery and the environmental arts organisation Cape Farewell. The editor of three anthologies, most recently *Ten: The New Wave* (Bloodaxe, 2014), Karen's poetry is published by Poems on the Underground, *The Poetry Review*, *Poetry London* and *Modern Poetry in Translation*, journals for which she also reviews. Her collection *An Aviary of Small Birds* is forthcoming from Oxford Carcanet.

Helen Mort was born in Sheffield and lives in Derbyshire. Her first collection of poetry, *Division Street* (Chatto, 2013), was shortlisted for the T.S.Eliot Prize and the Costa Prize.

MARY PATERSON is a writer and curator who works across visual art, text and performance. Mary's writing practice is driven by collaboration and dialogue, and operates between criticism, poetry and creative non-fiction. She is the co-founder of Open Dialogues, a writing collaboration which produces writing on and as performance. In 2014 she launches *Something Other*, an Arts Council, England funded research project exploring digital literature in relation to the live.

GARETH E. REES is the author of *Marshland: Dreams and Nightmares on the Edge of London* (Influx Press, 2013) a psychedelic voyage through East London's marshes. His spoken word album with chamber music ensemble, *Jetsam – A Dream Life of Hackney Marshes,* was released by Clay Pipe Music in 2013. He has penned numerous essays and short stories about walking, fantasy and our relationship to place.

GEMMA SELTZER is a writer working online, live and in print. Her digital writing projects include *5am London* (2012), collaborating with a photographer to document the city during the early hours, and *Look up at the Sky* (2011), charting the quiet parts of the Thames through walking and writing. She is the author of daily fiction blog *Speak to Strangers* (2009) about random interactions with Londoners, subsequently published by Penned in the Margins. Gemma was writer in residence for the Olympic torch relay and at Tate Modern, and has presented her work at the Venice Biennale.

CHRISSY WILLIAMS is a freelance editor who lives in London. Her pamphlet *Flying into the Bear* (HappenStance Press) was shortlisted for the Michael Marks Awards, and the *TLS* called it 'the most energetic, delightful collection you will read this year.' She has three other pamphlets, including *Epigraphs* (if p then q) and two collaborations with visual artists, *Angela* (Sidekick Books) and *The Jam Trap* (Soaring Penguin). She is director of the Poetry Book Fair and runs an informal poetry and comics workshop.

TAMAR YOSELOFF's most recent poetry collections are *The City with Horns* (Salt, 2011) and *Formerly* (Hercules Editions, 2012), a chapbook incorporating photographs by Vici MacDonald which was shortlisted for the Ted Hughes Award. She is also the author of two collaborative editions with the artist Linda Karshan and the editor of *A Room to Live In: A Kettle's Yard Anthology*. She lives in London, where she is a freelance tutor in creative writing. Her fifth collection, *The Formula for Night*, is due from Seren in 2015.